WHAT'S YOUR
PSYCHIC I.Q.?

WHAT'S YOUR PSYCHIC I.Q.?

HOW TO LISTEN TO YOUR INNER VOICE

AND LET IT GUIDE YOU TO A BETTER LIFE

MARTHA IVERY

PRIMA PUBLISHING

3000 Lava Ridge Court • Roseville, California 95661

(800) 632-8676 • www.primalifestyles.com

PRIMA PUBLISHING and colophon are registered trademarks of Prima Communications, Inc.

Illustrations by Neiel Cavin
Interior design by Knockout Design

All products mentioned in this book are trademarks of their respective companies.

Library of Congress Cataloging-in-Publication Data
Ivery, Martha.
   What's your psychic I.Q.? : how to listen to your inner voice and let it guide you to a better life / Martha Ivery.
      p. cm.
   Includes index.
   ISBN 0-7615-1479-1
      1. Parapsychology.   2. Psychic ability.   I. Title.
BF1031.I94 1998
133—dc21   98-50614
                                                                CIP

00 01 02 03 HH 10 9 8 7 6 5 4 3 2 1
Printed in the United States of America

How to Order
Single copies may be ordered from Prima Publishing, 3000 Lava Ridge Court, Roseville, CA 95661; telephone (800) 632-8676. Quantity discounts are also available. On your letterhead, include information concerning the intended use of the books and the number of books you wish to purchase.

Visit us online at www.primalifestyles.com

To my parents,
who are indeed a blessing

Contents

Introduction

My oncologist once told me I was a very sensitive person. It didn't dawn on me until a few years later what he meant by this. He was really talking about my psychic abilities, but he may not have known that.

When I was a young girl back in the late 1950s and early 1960s, people stayed away from me because I would tell them what was going to take place before it happened. I started learning about my psychic abilities when I was a child. They were just as natural a part of my life as breathing. I've had a Spirit Guide with me since I was five years old.

Sometimes my psychic energy is radiating through my energy field at such a high level that when I walk down the street car alarms will go off automatically, clocks will stop or their hands will turn rapidly, and all the electricity in the area will shut down.

This is very discouraging for me, especially when my computer won't work or my telephone just gives a slight ring and then doesn't work at all. My husband will give me one of those looks when the television or his electric razor turns off and on. I had to learn how to contain my energy and it is very hard to do, especially if you are not conscious of it. If you are not careful, your energy can make your life go awry. A major change for me as I discovered how to use my psychic abilities was learning to take guidance in many forms, including Spirit Guides. I do my own deep work constantly on this topic. My training methods have included traditional methods like Reiki and the study of Buddhism and the Four Noble Truths. I use many traditional training techniques such as discovering how to create joy in your life and helping others develop their psychic potential. This is done by believing in yourself and by taking heart. Our psychic energy is not gone; we have just temporarily lost track of it. Learning how to bring it back will be exciting. We owe it to ourselves to start recapturing it.

Remember that energy is a neutral force—a fire can cook a meal or burn down a city—and energy's intent returns to the sender. What you send out returns to you, for good or bad. Psychic energy, along with the ability and power to use it, is one of many endangered mysteries. The reason for this is that anything "psychic" is sacred. Indeed, it is sacred, but no longer is it secret or limited to a select few. I want to end this secret of the mysticism of our psychic nature and to bring it to those who need and want it.

You can fully embrace this remarkable inborn power by following the simple techniques in this book. Psychic energy will help you determine the events, emotions, and circumstances that make up your reality. It is a power we have had all our lives, but haven't even begun to use.

Spirituality is erupting faster than time itself. Psychic awareness is a part of what lies ahead for all of us in the new millennium.

PSYCHIC ABILITIES

Many people, almost all of us, are psychic whether we know it or not, some of us more than others. Psychic energy is natural, ubiquitous, useful, and a contribution to society. Your innate psychic energies are given to you at conception and birth for your use in your life. You can have a more positive relationship with your natural abilities.

I believe those of us who are more psychic than others have become that way because we practice using the psychic energy readily available to all of us. It is like a child learning how to walk. And by learning every day, a little at a time, everyone is able to learn about a world that has always been here, waiting for us to enter its dimension. Psychic energy is all around us and has been since the world began. Answers to any problems will be readily available to you when you learn how to apply your psychic energy.

Psychic abilities are related to creativity, wholeness, and self-confidence. ESP enhances life. You participate more in life, both in giving and receiving energy. We have a choice about what we plug into in life: drugs, pastimes, money, or good energy. When you have an electrical appliance you need to plug it into an electrical outlet to get it to work. Think of yourself as an electrical plug looking for an outlet. If you have no place to plug in, you are out of luck. Your life is going too fast, you have no time for anything or anyone—until one day you realize you need to find a place to plug your life into. We need to look where we are going.

Anything negative in this world is always, and I want to say that word again, *always* readily available to all of us, much more so than learning about our innate psychic energies. Lifting the veil on your abilities helps you plug into the right things. When you tap into the main line of the power plant you can dispel a lot of negativity. Students who exhibit the most ESP also score high on creativity. We are talking about an inner potential, not something that you either have in your makeup or not.

The effects of learning and the rebirth of "psychic energies" are life changing. Old emotions are released; you see life in a different perspective. It's walking from the physical realm to a spiritual realm. A new life, a new beginning. As in learning to walk, we can gradually develop and strengthen our abilities.

THIS BOOK

This book is a unique guide to exploring your potential. Learn what the word *psychic* really means. For people who want to learn about the sacredness of the psychic, we need to bring it to within their grasp. We no longer have the time or the luxury of studying with a private tutor or master/ guru/teacher. There are very few professing psychics who devote their lives to this sacred path. People learn mostly from reading books and "on-the-job training."

This book will help you develop the "gift" that everyone has—the gift to utilize the psychic energies within you. Truly you do not yet know what your natural abilities will do for you and how they will come to the fore in your life once you develop them a bit. The meaning of your life cannot help but change. To regain the part that has been lost requires your spiritual attention and a key to the sacred. Everyone must find the particular key to his or her own psychic abilities. We have practical exercises to help you find your key.

The teaching methods and exercises within this book are an integrated energy system. I don't believe there has ever been a book that teaches you how to become a "psychic" or to develop your hidden psychic abilities.

Your work will give meaning to a larger perspective of yourself. You will become more useful in solving the world's problems. When secrecy and mystification have been set aside and as the urgent need for the healing of our people and our planet grows, there will be a larger field for us to play upon with our newfound talents.

In the following pages, you will learn what this psychic energy really is, where it resides, and how to tap into it. You will also receive a very special invitation, but beware —if you accept it, you will never again see your personal expectations, your deepest desires, or your spiritual journey quite the way you do today. Reality itself will take on a different meaning. Are you prepared to embark on a journey to a whole new way of thinking, understanding, and living?

When your heart throbs with love or your stomach clenches in fear, you're in touch with "it." When a moment of quiet reflection brings the answer, the idea, the revelation you have waited for, you are experiencing power from within, your own psychic energy.

It is your true self—the part of you that is all-knowing, infinitely peaceful, and completely free. It is the self that knows where to go and what to do to heal your wounds, make real your dreams, and fulfill your true desires. It is your self that is immune to the sands of time and the winds of change, the part you've known the longest, yet may understand the least. It is your highest self, which is a truly remarkable power. Here are some of the benefits to discovering this self:

- With calm and ease you will be able to dissolve boundaries and limitations that fence in your spirit.

- You will have control over seemingly external forces, such as time, anxiety, and fear.

- You will come to know that your reality is simply clay in your hands.

If that sounds too good to be true, I understand. Through trial and error all my life, I have learned to tap into and use my psychic energies. We have all heard stories of people who defied medical diagnoses, lived decades longer than predicted, and recovered from "terminal" illnesses (I can vouch for that one myself). Your natural state is one of balance of mind, body, and spirit, which leads to well-being and happiness.

The key to unlocking this natural power is you. Reality and distractions get in the way of the "soft calls" from your deepest self. But you can learn to tune out the internal and external dialogue that bombards the inner self so you can hear what the most brilliant, open, and aware part of you has to say. Lay claim to what has been yours since the beginning of time.

Have you ever realized in conversation with a close friend or lover that there was a time when you have been in close proximity before, when you went to the same school, worked in the same building, attended the same New Year's Eve party, but didn't meet. Connecting with your own psychic energy can give you that same astonishment and wonder. You will remember the many times it brushed your hand, but you did not grasp it.

The straightforward information in this book will help you to do the following:

- *Eliminate negative emotions,* putting an end to feelings of doubt, disappointment, rejection, and failure; heal old hurts; and clear blocked emotions so you can rejoin the blissful current of life.

- *Trust your physical body,* and discover your own power to heal and take care of yourself.

- *Forge powerful connections* with community, environment, and all of creation. Living only for yourself limits the energy available to you.

- *Grow through intimacy,* and draw nourishment from inner energies.

- *Simplify your life automatically,* and eliminate chaos from the busiest life. Free up your energy reserves.

- *Develop more satisfying relationships.* See yourself as the person you truly are: a person of infinite worth and energy. Learn how to let an honest heart guide you.

- *Overcome addictions and compulsions.* Experience pleasure that surpasses intense addictions and quiets a troubled mind by learning how to contain your psychic energy.

- *Discover joy and happiness.* When you start to live your life at the level of psychic energy, you will use your power to continually renew your life.

Once you have mastered the lessons in this book—and reached the highest level of awareness of what you hold within you—your reality becomes so transformed that the less you do, the more you accomplish. The less you try to possess the more you get.

Now you can discover the silent place within you, the power of the universe that is constantly unfolding. This is my invitation to you. I promise that from the first moment you begin to act on the lessons given in this book, you will feel a marked shift in your perspective on the world around you. You will then see that this world is a place where the mind can physically and psychically change the body, where you think not just with your brain but with your entire body, where matter exists only as a swirling pattern of information, and where you can actively create your reality.

PART

I

THE SOURCE OF PSYCHIC ENERGIES

CHAPTER 1

Your Psychic Energy

Psychic energy is a life force in the body and in the universe. This force balances us in our environment. We can become aware of and manipulate this energy. We all have psychic energy; we just fail to recognize it because it's not taught to us at home or in schools. We all have access to the larger universe.

One simple way to begin to connect to this energy is by counting our blessings. This simple act can help us relax and appreciate our relationship with our environment and with the infinite. Some of us don't feel that seeing a beautiful sunset, or just *seeing,* is a blessing, but it is. Some of us don't feel that eating with a spoon or a fork is a blessing, but it is. And some of us don't even think that using a toilet regularly is a blessing, but it is.

Think about those who don't have these blessings, those who are blind, those who are in the hospital with a catheter, those who are in jails or prisons. We have so much, if we would just take the time to be thankful for the small things in life.

The best time to make a connection with our psychic energy is early in the morning; it seems to make the rest of the day more positive and you are able to perceive more about life's coincidences all day long. The more you connect to the Higher Power or God, the more psychic energy you receive, and the more psychic energy you have, the more psychic abilities you can perform.

You will blossom like a flower every day, and the meaning of your life will change. You will be able to see things in a different perspective. Material wealth, for instance, will not be important to you, as you can obtain it anytime you want in your lifetime. You will want to help others by giving away your energy, yet you will be receiving back more energy, positive and strong energy from your main line, which is God or whatever name you use. It's about time you made use of what God and the Cosmos gave you.

Every blade of grass, leaf, or petal; the air we breathe, the sunlight and its warmth; the aroma of a flower and the bark of a tree; insects and animals; nutrients from the earth such as zinc, copper, marble, quartz, and diamonds; herbs; human beings; water; dust particles; and man-made inventions like cars, trains, boats, and planes—everything comes from an energy source.

This realization is your first step in learning how you can utilize the innate psychic abilities that were given to each of us on the day we were conceived. Teach them to your children at a young age and by the time they are adults, and perhaps even before that, they will know many things before they happen. Your children can change their own destiny, perhaps even history.

The first concept is the circulation of the life force energy running through your body. One important key to the circulation of this energy is breathing, an act which brings about consciousness and without which there is no life. Our life force energy, which develops our psychic abilities, reconnects the link between the physical energy and spirit bodies. The intention to move our innate psychic energy is expressed when we attempt to do a healing, know things before they happen, or make objects move just by standing next to them.

Although all energy comes from Heaven and Earth, it is the energy force within us that needs to be controlled. Our life force is instilled in us at conception, and it is this energy that is stored in the space between the navel and the Belly Chakra (Door of Life), in front of the kidneys in the center of the body.

The energy channels enter our bodies and circulate throughout. Sometimes we can have an "overloaded" channel, as in the case of my electrical experiences. All of our channels that transport our psychic energy begin with a primary channel flanked by a pair of channels that move more energy in opposite directions. These channels follow the line of the spinal column vertically through our body. They branch to become the body's entire electrical "wiring" system. Branching from these primary channels are all the large and small channel lines (similar to our capillaries). These smaller channels of energy reach into the physical level. And then, divided further is the physical nervous system. This network of branching channels is the bridge between the etheric (emotional) and higher vibrational bodies.

VIBRATION CHAKRAS

Imagine your energy channels as several branches from the main tree, the Tree of Life. There are three primary channels of energy called Kundalini. The great channel running vertically through the body along the spinal column from the Crown to the Root Chakra is called the Sushumma. It is the connection between the energies of the Earth and the Universe and contains a neutral energy charge. On the physical level this is the spinal cord and central nervous system.

I believe when there is a disruption of energies in this channel through trauma or disease, energy flow can be restored or repaired somewhat through multiple "laying on of hands," directing energy that took a wrong turn in its proper channel. This energy transfusion is similar to a blood transfusion. The movement of energy in all channels is described as having a spiral shape, a pattern that often appears in nature. The discipline (which I sometimes don't have) of moving our energy is called opening the Kundalini in India, but it has other names in other cultures. Replenishing our energy or life force is a major goal in some parts of the world.

In India the process of replenishment consists of moving your energy upward from the Root to the Crown Chakra (see Figure 1). Once this energy reaches the crown, it is expected to release there or return along the pathway through which it came. In Asia the downward path is given as much attention as the upward movement. This dual approach results in fewer negative symptoms caused by the backlash of more energy than the body can handle.

In the Chinese practice ch'i-kung, where the energy pathway is directed in a circle rather than upward only, the goal is to use the life force for health and long life. Spiritual awakening then follows. Practicing the energy circle on a daily basis is said to cure diseases because it heals energy blockages and weaknesses anywhere in the body and brings new vibrant energy to all organs. By moving energy through multiple channels in opposite directions, any excess energy is safely stabilized.

What does this mean for you? It means you will be able to generate a vibrant energy flow through your entire body, and move it through your primary channels and branching energy pathways to the palms of your hands. With the "laying on of hands," or Reiki, you will be able to direct and increase the flow of your psychic energy.

The most important aspect to remember is that we are a sacred channel for the life force energy of God.

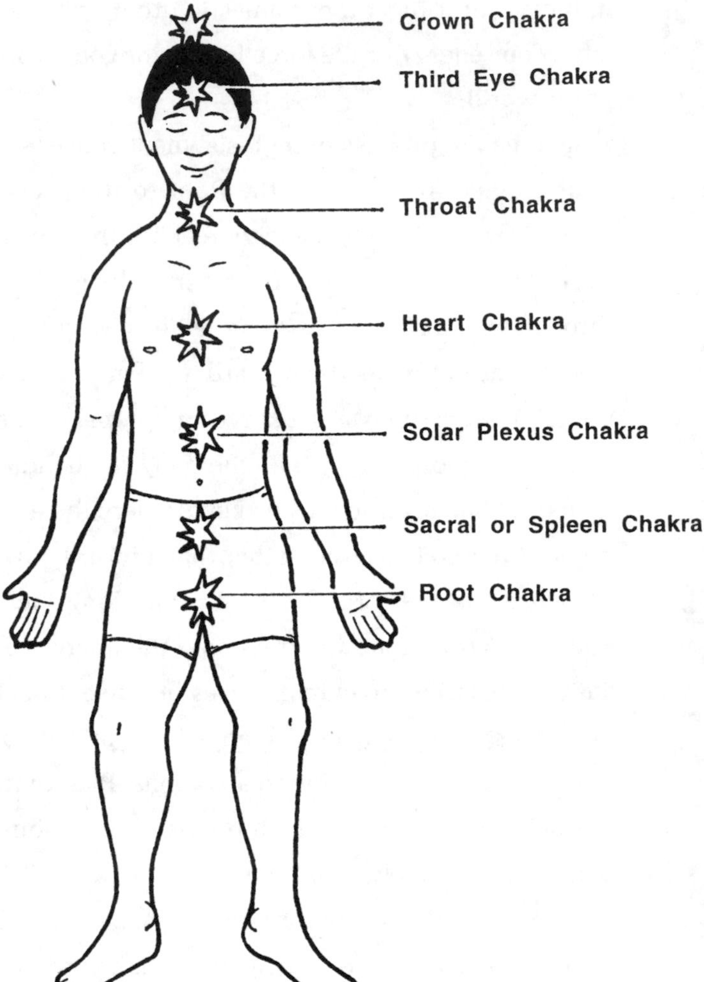

Figure 1. The Seven Chakras

MEDITATION

Your psychic energy, which has been dormant for years, can reconnect to the power plant through meditation. To meditate you have to be alone (outdoors if possible) and have no disturbances. Or you can be in your own room or any part of your home. During this meditation period, allow the mind and body to become one and be receptive to the soul's vibrations. I also value prayer to direct attention back to God, as well as to help others with the talents that emerge in the form of psychic abilities.

A tiredness will occur after your meditation period or anytime you connect one-on-one with God. You will find this to be true if you have laid your hands on someone who is in pain or when you draw upon the universal energy for any reason. When that happens, you must rest, sleep if you like. During your rest period, think about how peaceful and calm life really is; think about infinite love and all that there is for you.

Psychic abilities are a function of knowledge and skills developed and constructively applied. What we use is ours to keep. I encourage you to take a practical approach. We should look for our psychic abilities to appear first in those areas of life where some creative talent is already being used in service to others, and go from there. I consider this to be one part self-development at the spiritual, mental, and physical level; and one part service to others at the level of prayer and everyday interactions with others. In this way, one step at a time, balanced development is assured. Psychic abilities are not some new, superhuman power, but the natural expression of your soul.

Explore meditation and hypnosis, explore the Ouija board and automatic writing, explore your subconscious and superconscious; they will scale the heights and plumb the depths of your mind. Or abandon consciousness all together and take a nap, for in dreams we experience still other dimensions of our existence. And then, there is deep, dreamless sleep—the state of consciousness most naturally in harmony with the original, infinite mind.

PREPARATION FOR THE ENERGY EXERCISES

People have one of two beliefs about their psychic energy levels. One group believes that there is no such thing as having their own psychic energy field. The second group includes those who may believe there is truly an energy field, but they do not believe it can be seen. Fortunately, we are at a point where we can prove that there is an energy field and that it can be seen.

Most people only see or experience as much as is necessary or essential to them and their immediate, individual lives. People today are ignorant of the functions and activities of the physical body. There exists an attitude that we have physicians, so why take the time ourselves? Thus we give over our responsibilities and much of our innate power and control. When you are so casual about your own physical body and its energies, it is no wonder there is such strong prejudice against the even more subtle energies of life.

This section of exercises is designed to increase your awareness and perception of the more subtle fields around you. The exercises will help you feel and see the energy emanations of your body and help you understand their influences upon you. Practice and persistence with these exercises is the key.

The exercises are organized in a progressive manner. They begin simply so you can start to feel and experience some of the more subtle psychic energies, and they build to exercises that will assist you in not only feeling the energies but also actually seeing them as well.

Unfortunately, when it comes to our own psychic energy we are often dealing with a belief system. Regardless of scientific verification, if the belief is held that no such thing exists, the task of opening a new realization can be difficult. Most people grow up with little or no acknowledgment of the subtle energies of life. Any such experiences are attributed to an active imagination. These exercises will assist in breaking down those outworn, limiting thoughts and ideas; reawaken and expand the subtle perceptions that closed down in childhood; increase your sensitivity; and strengthen your visual awareness of the psychic energy within you.

The time frame in which results will be experienced varies from individual to individual. Persistence is the key. Initially, some exercises will be more successful than others. Do not become discouraged at any failure during first attempts to experience and see your psychic energy field. Remember: Seeing your psychic energy field is natural to all of us! The ability to do so has lain dormant for many years. You must begin to stretch those unused muscles and abilities slowly and persistently. If you follow through and do not let yourself become discouraged, you will be successful!

Although the exercises can be enjoyable, there is a serious side as well. Learning to see your psychic energy field is a commitment to yourself and to others. Approach the exercises with sincerity and keep in mind that you are embarking on a lifelong process that will enable you to know yourself and others more intimately. You are stepping out into areas that lead to sacred perceptions. Treat the process with respect.

The effects of the exercises are increased when you learn the skill of relaxed concentration. Trying too hard can block your progress. Learn to meditate and relax the body before the exercises. Performing a short, progressive relaxation before an exercise is beneficial. Take a few moments, close your eyes, and breathe deeply from the diaphragm. Focus on each part of your body, starting at your feet. Mentally send warm, relaxing feelings into that area of the body, progressing through each major muscle group, and culminating at the crown of your head.

Take your time with this practice. Close your eyes and employ deep, rhythmic breathing. You may wish to use soft music or environmental sounds to assist in relaxation.

The longer you focus on each part, the more relaxed you will be and able to concentrate. The more you are able to concentrate, the more sensitive you become to the energies around you.

Relaxation creates a hyperconscious condition, and you become hypersensitive. If you have ever been jarred from a daydream by a phone ringing or other loud noise, you have experienced one aspect of this condition. When you are relaxed, in an altered state of consciousness, you will experience outside energies more intensely. Noises will seem louder. Smells are stronger. Light and colors become brighter. Because of this, relaxation will assist you in perceiving the subtle energies of your psychic energy field more easily. Relaxation will amplify your perceptive abilities.

In the following exercise, you are simply working to become more sensitive to the subtle emanations surrounding your physical body. This exercise can be performed alone, but it can also be adapted to practicing with a friend or spouse.

Your hands are points where there is a greater degree of energy activity. There are a number of these spots throughout the body. Seven of these are associated with the traditional chakra system (Figure 1). Energy emanations are stronger around these areas of the body. Your hands, however, can become very sensitive to the subtle energies surrounding your body. They can be used to feel this energy

13

as well as to project it outward. It is this ability that is known as the "king's touch," "the laying on of hands," the etheric or therapeutic touch in healing.

You will begin your exercises with the hands because they are the easiest means of detecting the subtle energies of your psyche. As you increase your sensitivity to this aspect of yourself, you will increase sensitivity in other areas as well.

EXERCISE 1
Experiencing Your Subtle Energies

1. Begin by making yourself comfortable in a seated position. Perform a relaxation exercise to prepare.

2. Rub the palms of your hands together briskly for fifteen to thirty seconds. This helps activate their overall sensitivity.

3. Extend your hands a foot to a foot and a half in front of you, the palms facing each other. Hold the hands about two feet apart.

4. Slowly move the hands toward each other. Bring them as close to each other as you can without touching.

5. Draw them slowly back to about six inches apart. Slowly repeat this in and out movement.

6. As you perform this exercise, you may experience a feeling of pressure building or you may have other sensations. There can be a sense of rubberiness, tickling,

pressure, or even a thickness building between your hands. You may feel warmth or coolness. You may even experience a pulsating feeling.

7. Now take a few minutes to define what you are feeling. Do not worry about whether you are imagining it or that it may feel different from what others have experienced; that is okay. Remember, you have your own unique psychic energy field frequency, so you can experience it differently. Only what *you* experience matters.

8. This exercise assists in developing concentration. It also assists in helping you recognize that your psychic energy does not stop at skin level. You may wish to write down in a notebook your impressions and experiences with this exercise so you can compare them later with what you experience as you develop this ability further. Keeping a record will help you to recognize your progress in experiencing subtle energies around your body.

9. Once you have completed this exercise, you will want to take it a step further. Bare your weaker arm. Hold your dominant arm about a foot and a half above your bared forearm.

10. Slowly lower your hand toward the forearm. Pay attention to anything that you might feel. How close do you come to the forearm before you can feel the energy from it? The feeling may be one of pressure, heat, coolness, etc., much like what you experienced between your hands. It may not be as strong, but you should be able

to feel it. If you cannot, slowly repeat the exercise. Remember that you are reawakening your ability to consciously be aware of the subtle energies around you.

AWARENESS OF OUTSIDE ENERGIES

An old occult axiom states, "All energy follows thought." Wherever your thoughts are focused, so are your psychic energy patterns. Your psychic energy adjusts its frequency in accordance with your thoughts. If you are focusing upon an important meeting, your psychic energy will adjust its frequency to one of a serious vibration, a frequency appropriate to the occasion. If you are looking forward to a vacation, by the time it arrives, your psychic energy field will have adjusted itself to a more relaxed, casual frequency. Whether you are watering your plants or thinking of someone special, you will learn to perceive and control your psychic energy field to become more aware of the thoughts you project throughout your day.

You are exposed to the influence of extraneous energies constantly. These can impinge upon your psychic energy field and affect your balance. These energies can be anything from anger and lust to the pressure to buy. They can be the energies of warmth and friendship or those of manipulation. The more sensitive you become to your own psychic energy field, the more you can recognize and control what energies you allow in and out.

We all have had experiences where we walk into a room and feel that a certain "something," such as a fight or argument, has just occurred. The room has a distinct "feel." The air seems thick and tense. We become edgy ourselves. There are many such energy residues and projections that are not as easily detectable. These can influence and affect you easily if you do not increase your awareness and sensitivity to them.

In the following exercise you will work to increase your awareness of how outside energies can affect you. As you increase your psychic energy sensitivity, you can block those energies that create stress and direct those that heal.

EXERCISE 2
Sending and Feeling Energy Patterns

1. Make yourself comfortable in a seated position. Take a few minutes to relax. You may wish to keep your eyes closed through this exercise, but it is not necessary.

2. Hold one hand palm upward. Point the index finger of your other hand into your open palm. Your finger should be three to six inches away from your other hand.

3. Take nice, deep, slow breaths. As you breathe in and out, imagine your pointed index finger building energy in your hand.

4. After several minutes, slowly rotate your finger in a small circle. Visualize a spiraling stream of energy. Don't worry about whether you are imagining it as you are working to prove that energy does follow your thoughts.

5. Pay attention to what you feel within the palm of your hand. Just as in the previous exercise, the feeling may vary from person to person. You may feel a circle of warmth unfolding and forming in your hand. You may also experience a thickness, a pressure, or a tingling in the form of a small circle within your palm. Sometimes closing your eyes at this point can help you feel the sensation more strongly. The more you project and focus the energy with your mind and out through your index finger, the stronger the sensation will become.

6. Having worked with the palm of your hand, next perform this same activity upon your naked forearm. Visualize and send the energy out in small spirals to impact upon your forearm. Observe what you feel. You will find that with time and practice the kind of sensation you experience will remain much the same; what will vary is the intensity. Through exercises such as this, you can train yourself to recognize those feelings that something is subtly affecting your energy field.

7. Slowly lower your hand toward your forearm. How close do you come to your forearm before you can feel the energy from it? Remember that the feeling may be one of pressure, heat, coolness, etc. It will feel much like what you experienced between your hands. It may not be as strong, but you should be able to feel it. Remember that you are reawakening your ability to be consciously aware of the subtle psychic energies around you.

8. This exercise can be performed with another individual. Have the other person stand with his back to you. Hold your hand six to twelve inches from your partner. Slowly direct the psychic energy from your hand to the other person's back, just as you did with your own arm. Trace simple geometric shapes such as a circle, square, or triangle. Keep repeating the movement with your hand and concentrate as you project the energy.

9. Have the other person try to identify the shape that is being drawn on him. Pay attention to what is felt and compare it to the sensations experienced in the previous exercises.

10. Gradually increase the distances. How far away can you get from your arm and still feel the circles upon it? How far can someone stand behind you and project on your back psychic energy you are able to identify? Does it feel differently when the distances are extended? Note your responses. This exercise increases your overall sensitivity to subtle energies and their effects upon your own psychic energy field.

EXERCISE 3

Detecting Intrusions in Your Psychic Energy

For this exercise, you will work to increase your sensitivity to when outside energies touch, interact with, or intrude upon your own psychic energy field. You will need a partner for this exercise.

1. Take a few minutes to relax, then stand with your back to a wall with your eyes closed.

2. Your partner should stand on the other side of the room.

3. Your partner steps forward silently and slowly until you can feel her with your psychic energy space. The partner moves one step at a time, pausing after each step. It's like playing "Mother May I."

4. Keep your eyes closed and feel the room with your mind and your psychic energy alone. You may wish to place cotton in your ears and use a blindfold so there are no auditory or visual clues. Pay attention to how the room feels before you start. Note any changes you begin to feel.

5. How close does your partner get to you before you can feel her presence? What sensations are you experiencing? Can you feel when your partner moves to one side or the other? Add a third or fourth person. Can you feel their energies more easily if they move closer together?

6. This is a good exercise to experiment with and have fun as well. Don't be afraid to adapt and change it. Mark a spot six to eight feet out from you before you start. As you close your eyes, stay focused on that spot. Can you feel when your partner crosses the invisible line? Do your energies feel stronger than when you are alone?

You are learning that you extend beyond the physical body. You are developing greater sensitivity to your entire psychic energy field. As you increase this feeling of sensitivity, you will increase visual perception as well.

THE LARGER CONNECTION

When we start to sense the source of energy, we begin to understand its complexity. It teaches us about ourselves—to help others who cannot access it, to love, to heal, to do for mankind—and it gives us the earth, and everything we have and take for granted.

Whenever you do *anything,* it takes energy. To write these words took energy from my hand to the pen; this is the type of energy we can understand, but what about psychic energy? It's only when you can fully comprehend or understand it that you will be able to visualize it. Where does it come from and how do we use it? Psychic energy is just another one of our senses, unused, not brought to its full potential. Perhaps the veil that covers God's truth is the lack of use of our innate psychic energy.

Of course, there's that common-sense attitude that must be applied, but even when common sense doesn't compute or register in our life's reactions, we can use our psychic energy or abilities to solve any mystery, like finding missing people.

For those who are just beginners, like a newborn babe in learning about psychic abilities (as most of us are), I am going to list a few suggestions you will need to practice at your leisure. Try to draw from the main line at least twice a week, more if you can, and on a regular basis. The main line is from your Creator. First of all, you must know in your heart, mind, soul, and body that God or whatever name you choose is your main line, your Maker, your infinite source of love and understanding.

How to Access the Energy Flow

Plan a timeline of exercise that will allow for gradual development. The process of following the energy within us is accessed through the compassionate state of mind that brings us happiness. It is one of the fundamental beliefs that not only do we inherently possess the potential for compassion, but the basic or underlying nature of human beings is gentleness. It is the nature of all sentient beings to be gentle and not aggressive. This state of mind, present in all human beings, is completely untainted by negative emotions or thoughts. And this is the beginning of learning how to go through the process of development of our psychic abilities.

If we look at the pattern of our existence from an early age until death, we can see the way we are fundamentally nurtured by the affections of others. It begins at birth, as does the psychic energy within us. We cannot ignore the fact that conflicts and tensions exist, but by learning how to control our own internal energies using our individual minds, we can act on many circumstances before they happen. The ultimate solution to any conflict is to return to our basic understanding, our basic underlying psychic powers instilled at birth.

There are three methods for accessing energy. The first is to regularly tap into the main line of energy in the universe, which has been discussed. The second way is the ancient Greek advice "Know thyself," which is a good suggestion for developing psychic ability. To know thyself exacts a price; yet it also offers a reward. The price is that we must bear the burden of responsibility for who we are. We can't blame others. The reward is found in self-acceptance and the freedom to be who we are. The third method is meditation (and prayer) and dreams, which are described in more detail in chapter 6, "Advanced Tools: Meditation As a Pathway" and in chapter 7, "Advanced Tools: Dreams As a Pathway."

I believe that the very purpose of our life is to seek happiness. We are all seeking something better in life and move toward happiness. All feelings come from energy moving. As with electricity, there must be a main power plant that supplies us. Energy comes in the form of feelings, actions, behaviors, solid matter, etc. Our most important energy is that which processes thoughts and deeds.

For instance, if you maintain the feeling and actions of compassion, then an inner door automatically opens. Through that door, you can communicate more easily with others and with God. The biggest problems in our daily life are those things we need to face. The truth is inevitable. And the truth of our psychic energy can help us. Once you face the truth of your own abilities, you have the ability to create things beyond what comes by chance. How can we start? We start here at the beginning.

PREPARING TO TAP INTO
THE MAIN LINE
Make the Psychic Connection
Part of Your Daily Life

Learn to cooperate. This may sound too easy to be useful, but it is profound in its simplicity. Cooperation means co-ordination with others. To learn to cooperate, we must change our behavior to harmonious behavior. We must "get on the level" of basic reality and oneness. Cooperation builds consciousness. Our opportunities to choose are endless, and what we choose indicates our attitude toward basic reality and oneness. Learning how to choose to coop-erate takes patience. We want our psychic abilities now, to have telepathic impressions now. Perhaps we can compare it to the youthful desire to fall in love and think that having sex proves that love exists. Only through experience, when we are older, do we appreciate the true connection and un-derstand that sex is about *making* love. In much the same way, psychic awareness and ability and tapping into the main line are about the consciousness of oneness. And co-operation is how we get there. As we train for psychic abil-ity, we need to work on cooperativeness, empathy, and loving respect for others.

Develop Unity with the Main Line

Become one with the world. Imagine you have no head. That's right, look at the world around you and pretend that you have no head. Imagine that your body stops at your shoulders. You are no longer seeing with your eyes or your rational mind. Let the world you see take the place of your head. Now the world is your head! This odd experiment is about to take you into an altered state of consciousness and is meant to help you experience the world in a new way. Practice it a bit and have patience. Notice that although you have no head, you still have awareness of the world. So where is that awareness? Can you locate it? Your situation will change from the normal state of "I have awareness" to "Awareness is." Welcome to the reality of awareness, of "mind-at-large."

Now forget about your head and open yourself to the world. The world then joins you, and you become *one* with the world. This is tapping into the main line. You are still aware of individual objects because your head no longer blocks off the world from you. When we perceive ourselves as apart, we feel free to walk about in the world, but the downside is that we do feel separate and in need of protection to survive. We feel alienated inside our own heads. When we lose the head, we are somehow more connected to the world.

Astral travel. Another way of thinking about tapping into the main line is to look at the unity of mind and matter. Mind and matter are aspects of one reality. When we accept this and understand that our sensory impressions are not all there is to "reality," then we are able to "tour" the oneness. This is accomplished by leaving the body during sleep or deep meditation. When you have practiced enough, you can visit other places on earth and persons living and dead.

Using gemstones. Crystals definitely help me to connect with psychic energy around me and to obtain more of it through the main line. Crystals can be rose quartz, amethyst, diamond, amber, malachite, emerald, garnet, etc. Violet gemstones address the highest spirituality and white colors are the dissolvers of limitations. Soft pink and sky blue connect us with our heartfelt emotions. Garnet aligns and harmonizes and blue onyx is the gemstone for self-control and inspiration. Gemstones keep us in balance and our energy centers (chakras) attuned. Earth minerals can give us a lot of energy. If you put them in a bowl and touch them with your fingertips, you receive the ultimate pacifier for stress. These treasures from the earth can draw energy to you.

EXERCISE 4
Sample Meditation

When you combine your energy with focus of your essence on oneness, you create a phenomenon called synergism. This is true for all meditation. Meditation is like the daydreaming we all do every day, except that it is focused on oneness. In meditation we are trying to increase our psychic energy to a level where we have access to it anytime.

1. Find a peaceful place where you won't have any disturbances. If you are in your home, turn off the phone or unplug it. You should be alone in the house. Make yourself comfortable. Sit on a soft pillow and open the windows to let the sun and fresh air in; or if you are in the

city, close the windows and sit in silence. I like to walk in the woods and listen to the sounds of nature.

2. Take a few deep breaths. Raise your arms over your head, palms facing the heavens. Direct your attention there. Embrace yourself with your arms. Focus your energy on the larger energy. If you practice this with sensitivity, you will be aware of a spiritual presence around you. Guidance and answers to questions will come to you spontaneously.

3. As you end your session, be thankful. Close your eyes, touch up toward heaven with your palms and bring them down to your sides. Take another deep breath and open your eyes.

4. You will feel relaxed, stress will be gone, and you will feel new and enlightened, ready to start your day anew.

HOW TO SEE ENERGY FIELDS

Seeing your psychic energy is more physical than it is metaphysical. Anyone can learn to see his or her energy level, but interpreting what is seen is the difficult task and it involves more of the intuitive and metaphysical aspects of our human condition.

There are two ways of seeing your psychic energy field or level: intuitively and objectively. Either way of perceiving is as effective as the other, as long as what is seen is interpreted correctly. Both can be effective tools for insight, although physically perceiving the psychic field helps keep the "doubting Thomas" aspect of your consciousness out of your way.

Intuitive Seeing

In the intuitive method the psychic field is viewed within your mind's eye rather than through your physical eyes. It is learning to relax and visualize the individual within your mind. You must then ask your intuitive self about the energy of this internal energy field.

More often than not, these intuitive perceptions of the psychic field are as close and as accurate as the physical perceptions, if they are interpreted correctly. Thus one way of perception is not any better or effective than any other.

These intuitive perceptions of the psychic energy field are easier to observe in someone else than in yourself. It is easy to delude yourself and picture what you want to see within your own psychic energy field rather than what is actually there.

It is always good to have some kind of confirmation or backup for your intuition. The use of a dowsing rod or pendulum, which will be described in chapter 2, "Tools of the Psychic Trade," provides a means of objectively verifying your intuitive perceptions.

Objective Seeing

Physical perception provides you with a more tangible awareness of the subtle energy fields. Anyone can learn to objectively see his or her own psychic energy field. It is an ability that is natural to everyone. Most children can easily pick up on their own energy field, but they are not taught to recognize it for what it is. For instance, when a child sees a rainbow, he is actually seeing an energy field of light, dust, and the sun's rays. Or he may say, "Mommy, why are you so blue today?"

It is not unusual for parents to comment about the colorful imagination of a child when the child refers to subtle impressions or awareness. The child is often programmed by parents and society to believe that such perceptions are imaginary. As this occurs the child closes down and the innate ability to perceive subtle energies atrophies. This ability can be reawakened and redeveloped, however, no matter how long it has lain dormant.You can train your eyes to take in and translate more of the light spectrum. To understand how this works, you must understand how your eyes work, particularly the pupil, iris, and retina. The next chapter contains exercises to train the eyes.

Even with all the scientific verification, there will still be people who doubt they can ever see their psychic energy field. For those individuals, I often recommend an exercise that helps prove its existence and your ability to see it. This is the Tree Exercise.

EXERCISE 5
Seeing Tree Energy

1. Lie back in an open area of grass on a warm, cloudless day.

2. As you lie there, look at the distant trees.

3. Let your eyes run from the base of the trees to the top.

4. Gaze at the line the tree tops make against the blue sky. Don't force your gaze. Just relax.

5. Try to take in as much of the sky as you can. Let yourself relax into a soft focus, like that daydream look of staring off into nothingness.

6. As you do this, you will be aware of a soft haze that follows the outline of the tree tops against the blue sky, a diaphanous color, lighter than the blue of the sky beyond.

7. This phenomenon is most strongly visible in the spring when the sap and life force of trees are activated, and new growth and energy surge from the roots to the top branches. This is part of the psychic energy of the trees.

Tools of the Psychic Trade

The subconscious mind communicates through the nervous system. Because your own psychic energy field extends in all directions around you, it is sensitive to all that occurs in your environment. The conscious mind is usually only aware of what it is focused on and what is experienced through the five senses. If you look only to the five senses for information, you can easily miss the subtle plays of energy within your life. The subconscious mind, on the other hand, is aware of all energy interactions with your own field, even those beyond the five physical senses. These interactions are assimilated and can be accessed and brought into conscious awareness through meditation, hypnosis, and other techniques and tools for heightened consciousness.

To understand this fully, you must understand more of how the subconscious mind functions, as opposed to the way the conscious mind works. The conscious mind is the seat of organized brain activity. It controls sense perception and expression. When you are consciously focused upon an activity, your brain emits electrical waves. Beta brain wave is a term commonly used to describe the wave pattern emitted in consciously directed activities. Because you have become overidentified with your intellectual faculties, you either ignore the subtle perceptions of life or miss them entirely.

An alpha brain wave pattern occurs during relaxed states. This brain wave has a frequency of about ten cycles per second. The more relaxed you become, the slower the brain wave pattern and the more sensitive you become. Only about ten percent of your body and brain activity is consciously controlled activity. Thus it follows that if you are to reawaken the more subtle perceptions that register within you, you must learn to relax to access the subconscious mind.

The subconscious mind directs the autonomic nervous system. This system regulates the functions of the vital organs and involuntary muscles, including those in your eyes. For instance, the skin is a highly sensitive organ, and it has sensitivity to subtle waves of energy outside our body. These perceptions and messages can be recognizable through more of a conscious awareness of our energy emittance.

Here is a list of aids for our work:

1. Relaxation

2. Meditation

3. Dowsing rod

4. Pendulum

5. Breathing

6. Crystals

7. Eye training

8. Altered states of consciousness such as trance, hypnosis, mental telepathy, and spirit guides.

We have already discussed relaxation and meditation and will do so again later in this book. Right now let's discuss some material aids. There are many new electronic devices that can measure the energy field around the human body. Unfortunately, the average individual cannot afford most of them. This does not mean that we can't determine the size of our own psychic energy fields. We can still measure the size and strength of them with a high degree of accuracy with devices that anyone can make and use.

These devices are part of the science of radiesthesia. Radiesthesia is dowsing or divining to measure the strength of a particular radiation. It is a system for translating unrecognized nervous system responses to subtle energies into something tangible and visible. The two most common tools of radiesthesia are the dowsing rod and the pendulum. Both of these devices help you communicate with different levels of your mind that recognize the subtle energy fields you interact with.

Dowsing rods and pendulums are tools for communicating with your subconscious mind. The subconscious is aware of every interaction with outside energies, no matter how subtle. Through these tools, which are extensions of your eyes, you open greater powers of perception. Dowsing rods and pendulums are links between the nervous system (and the subconscious mind working through it) and those energy fields you interact with.

The histories of both methods are ancient. Although often thought of only as tools for psychics, the dowsing rod and the pendulum are employed in many traditionally conservative arenas of life. They have been used in wartime to detect underground mines and tunnels. Some utility companies train repairmen in their use so that only the appropriate lines are dug up when repairs are necessary. Although some would scoff at their use, traditional scientific equipment and methods are continually verifying the accuracy of dowsing rods and pendulums

Your higher consciousness or intelligence communicates with you through your nervous system, sending you signals. Radiesthesia devices amplify those signals of communication. You thus open further channels of sensitivity to those subtle energies of life.

DOWSING RODS

You may know the dowsing rod, or divining rod, which is used by farmers to find water. Some contractors use a divining rod, which is made of a branch from a pear tree or a peach tree and looks like the capital letter Y.

The divining rod searches for the energies in the earth and in most cases the first thing it finds is water, which is a great conductor of energy. You, too, can participate in such interactions with your environment. These rods can help you to link with those parts of yourself that are aware of this interaction.

When most people think of dowsing, they picture a man walking in a field holding the upper bars of a Y-shaped tree branch, trying to locate water or minerals. However, dowsing rods have a much greater application. A good dowser can not only locate subtle energy fields, but he can also find the answers to many questions.

Dowsing rods provide a link to your more intuitive side. They are an extension of your eyes. Many psychics use this method to find missing people, because the dowsing rods provide visual clues that you can recognize more easily. The rods have no special quality of their own. They are simply tools to heighten your sensitivity.

Many materials have been used as dowsing rods. The traditional peach branch is the most commonly known, but anyone can make a set of dowsing rods which can be just as effective. It is a simple task. About half of those who attempt it pick up the ability immediately. Others may have to practice for awhile, but anyone can become skilled at dowsing.

EXERCISE 6
How to Make and Use a Divining Rod

1. Take an ordinary metal clothes hanger and make two cuts in it at the designated spots (see Figure 2).

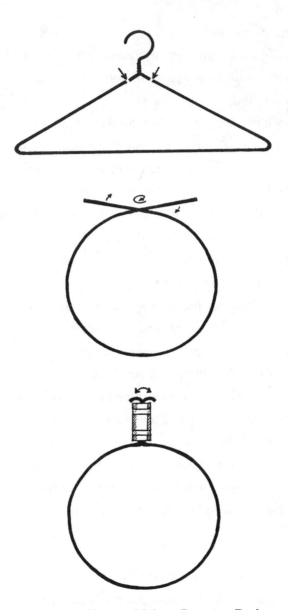

Figure 2. How to Make a Divining Rod

2. Bend the sides of the coat hanger to make a loop. Connect the ends of the wires by twisting them together about one and a half inches from the ends.

3. Next, take a piece of thin cardboard, three inches square, and roll it up into a small cylinder that can slide over the vertical part of the rod. Make the cardboard as stiff as you can and still roll it. It should be loose. Then, tape the cardboard into that rolled position.

4. Place the rolled-up cardboard over the twisted ends of wire. This will be the handle for your dowsing rod. Make sure that at least one inch of the vertical bar sticks out of the handle.

5. Take the part of the wire ends that extend out of the cardboard handle and bend them over so that the handle cannot slide off when the rod is used in an upright position.

6. Repeat steps one through five, making yourself a pair of dowsing rods. When finished, the rods should swing freely in the handles. They should feel comfortable in your hands.

7. You may wish to place a small weight at the end of the handle closest to the loop to help stabilize it. A small fishing sinker can be effective.

8. Once the dowsing rod is completed, hold it in your hand by the handle. Swing the horizontal bar around to make sure it has freedom of movement.

When you are looking for a missing person, take a piece of that person's clothing and hang it loosely across the top of the dowsing rods. Then, go in an area where you think that person was last or may be at this time. You can also look for a lost object this way. I know it sounds crazy, but you may find that what you are looking for is not far from where the rods are leading you. It is then that you will become acquainted with your old self. Your innate ability to use your psychic powers will finally awaken, and you can use them to your full potential.

PENDULUMS

Pendulums operate similarly to dowsing rods. Rather than a Y-shaped branch, the pendulum is more like what Edgar Allan Poe wrote about in his story "The Pit and the Pendulum."

The dowsing rod is usually considered the forerunner to the pendulum, which works along the same principle. The pendulum simply interacts with a particular energy field. It operates on bioelectrical principles and, like the dowsing rod, gives no answers itself.

When our energy level is high, the pendulum will move. When we are sleeping or at rest, it will move only a subtle fraction of a centimeter or not at all.

Making your own pendulum is easy to do. You can use objects found around your home or you can purchase them in a variety of stores. Buttons, crystals, and rings are commonly used as part of the pendulum. The best objects to use are round, cylindrical, or spherical. Attach your object to a thread, string, small chain, etc. The pendulum is hung freely from the end of the chain, and its movements provide answers and input to subtle energy awareness. It is actually an amplifier.

Learning to use the pendulum is easy. It requires only a little time and practice in a quiet place. It also requires the ability to relax. You must learn to keep emotions out of the pendulum process as they will short-circuit the electrical field of your psyche.

EXERCISE 7

Learning to Use a Pendulum

1. On the cardboard, draw a circle and write the words *yes* on the top and bottom of the circle and *no* on the right and left sides.

2. The first step in learning how to use the pendulum is to get the feel of it. Sit at a desk or table, making yourself comfortable. Have your feet flat on the floor and rest your elbow on the surface of the desk.

3. Hold the pendulum by its chain using your thumb and forefinger. Simply let the pendulum hang for a minute or two.

4. Now begin to gently circle it clockwise over the cardboard.

5. Hang the pendulum over the middle of the circle on the cardboard. You will see the pendulum swing either

vertically or horizontally by itself. At this point, you are simply becoming comfortable with its feel and the energy within you is doing all the work in moving it.

6. You can begin to do some experimentation with this. The most minute muscle movement will make the pendulum swing. You can cause the pendulum to swing without making any deliberate efforts. Allow the pendulum to hang still. Think to yourself, "Swing clockwise." Visualize this. Do not swing it yourself. Do it all with thought. When the pendulum begins to swing, think to yourself, "Stop." And you will see it come to a dead stop.

7. Ask a question while the pendulum is hanging still. This will test that it is not simply mind over matter. Ask, "Have I ever lived before?" If the answer is *yes,* the pendulum will move up and down in a vertical line. If *no,* it will move sideways or horizontally.

8. You must learn to ask *yes* and *no* questions. Don't ask it questions that need long drawn-out answers. You will not get a conversation out of the pendulum.

You can do this as often as you feel necessary to develop your psychic abilities. By practicing, you will be able to read other people's minds and know what they are going to say before they say it.

You must teach yourself to respond to impulses of immediate thoughts. You are telling the pendulum what kind of feedback it should give to you, and this is what you want to do with your own mind. Simply using the pendulum is the most effective way to bring more psychic energy and power to your needs at will.

With this exercise you are establishing communication between your innate psychic abilities and those who aren't using their psychic abilities or have lost them through ignorance.

It is important to keep the emotions out of the asking process. Some people will not relax and thus the pendulum responds only the way they want it to. If you relax and stay as unemotional as possible, the responses will become very accurate. The more you keep the conscious mind out of the process, the stronger the perceptions will become. Remember that alpha brain wave patterns, which occur when you are relaxed, will make you very sensitive to any psychic energy interactions within your own energy field.

BREATHING

Breathing is another method to open the channel to our intuitive inner self. Most of the time we do not pay attention to our breathing. It is automatic.

EXERCISE 8
Breathing Exercise

1. For a moment pay attention to your breathing. When you first notice it, you have the sensation that you are controlling the timing of inhalation and exhalation.

2. Try to relax for a moment, then gently observe your breathing and see if you can observe it without controlling it.

3. If you relax and are patient enough, you will gradually begin to witness your breathing as it happens all by itself, the way it happens all the time on its own when you are not paying any attention to it. Observing your breathing without interfering with it is an ancient form of meditation.

4. If you practice you will find that during exhalation you let go and become very relaxed, and breathing in you witness the mystery of inhalation. The word *inspire* is used to describe the intake of breath and it may give you a clue about inspiration as it is used in creativity. The processes are related.

CRYSTALS—PSYCHIC ENERGY TRANSDUCERS

How do the patterns of vibrations of the fourth dimension, such as thoughts, ideas, and images, interact with the brain and the body of the three-dimensional world? How do the infinite and the finite interact? Mental vibrations can "reach" from one person to the next because they transcend time and space. The brain resonates vibrations. It can translate vibrations of the fourth dimension into activities going on with the body and it can also do the reverse. For example, just to test yourself on this, when you pick up on another person's emotional state, the emotions are visceral, gut reactions of the body; yet, by way of vibrations of the fourth dimension, how is this accomplished?

Have you ever walked into a room full of people and for some unknown reason said to yourself, "I have to get out of here." Or perhaps you met someone and you just couldn't stand to be around him or her. Or you are walking down the street and you spontaneously sense someone behind you.

Animals have more sensory vibrations or psychic energy than we humans. They can pick up on the weather faster than we can with a satellite, and they can sense danger and death. If a dog howls throughout the night and day facing toward a certain area, be forewarned that someone or another animal is going to die or is already dead.

You may recall the old crystal radio sets. Through what seems like a magical process that scientists call the "piezoelectric effect," the crystal can transform the electromagnetic vibrations of radio waves into the physical vibrations of sound. We have a transformer in our body, an interconnected system of crystal known as the endocrine system.

The word *crystal* is an apt metaphor: The endocrine system functions like a system of crystal transducers, an electrical engineering term for a component that transforms energy from one form to another.

In the beginning, the soul's journey into the creation of bodies corresponded to the earth's formation, from a gaseous event into a solid planet. Crystals were formed within the earth's core. As souls were swimming within this cosmic brew, they projected their psychic energies into the developing crystals. As a result, the evolution of the body's psychic energy system became a development of the earth's crystalline deposits. In this way, the endocrine system corresponds to the earth's crystals. The soul's body and the earth are highly interdependent, historically and functionally.

You can test yourself on how well crystals work for your energy level. There are many types of crystals, each with its own energy balance. I am going to list for you the ones I am most familiar with and give you their properties. In the short exercise that follows, you can find out which ones work for you.

The crystal, itself an illuminating beam, intensifies through its many facets. It is skillfully fashioned in many shapes—star, moon crescent, circle, triangle, and square—and creates an aurora borealis effect when suspended in a window or in front of any light source. The many spectrums of color that are thrown around the room represent the chakra system.

Rose Quartz

The rose quartz comes in the exact color it describes, rose, and it looks like a stone. However, it has many more energetic properties than a stone. It comes with many positive energy gyrations. Placing it in a room will give you positive energy.

Cabochon

Searching for balance in your life? The cabochon crystal has a soothing and calming influence. This gemstone is actually a polished stone or any gem. It can be worn as jewelry or carried in a pocket with other stones that give you energy.

Serpentine

Serpentine is found in Connemara (marble) and iolite. This gemstone can be hung in your room to ward off harm.

Garnet

The garnet gemstone is a purifier, which cleans your energy field. If you wear it all day, you will be more in touch with your psychic self.

Tourmaline

This is an alternative to the diamond. It is associated with good luck and is deep green in color. It can be found as a polished stone and proclaims independence.

Citrine

This gemstone detoxifies your energy field. Citrine channels your energy toward success.

Amethyst

Amethyst is a meditation enhancer. If you wear it while meditating, you can feel its emittance. It is also a good stress releaser.

Cobalt

This crystal is deep blue. This color is an energizer and a divinatory tool. Cobalt can be used as a crystal ball.

Turquoise

Turquoise is the stone of friendship. It gives off a unique energy variation and is the gemstone of creative expression.

Malachite

This green stone is a stress reducer. It dispels apprehensions, distractions, and negative energy.

EXERCISE 9

How to Increase Your Energy Level with a Crystal

1. Place a crystal, such as amethyst or diamond, or some fairy dust (crushed crystal) around your windowsill in your bedroom. What happens next?

2. When you sleep the crystal on the windowsill will bring memories of before you were born into your subconscious; sometimes you can actually remember your dream. It will be more like a science fiction dream if you can remember it, but it is a special dream formed by the crystals and the psychic energies that emit from your body.

3. If you are ill and place a crystal in the room with you, your psychic energies will automatically flow with the crystal's energies promoting good health back to you.

Today, there is much interest in the use of crystals for healing and psychic development. The interest is appropriate as it expresses the recollection of this association of crystals with the "crossover point," the interface between the sensory world and the soul's psychic reality. What happens at the crossover? We all know our body is atomic particles in patterns. It is through these patterns of psychic energy that the physical processes became one being.

EYE TRAINING

Below are some exercises that will help you develop your eyes and strengthen their muscles. In the first exercise you will strengthen the muscles, particularly in the iris, and learn to adjust the amount of light you allow through your pupil to the retina. This ability can be developed to the point where you can discern subtle light emanations that you don't normally perceive.

These exercises will strengthen your eyes so that brighter color vision occurs along with more subtle light detection. As with all physical exercises, you should begin slowly and easily. You do not want to strain yourself or the muscles you are developing.

Have you ever noticed a flash of light in the corner of your eye? Or do you ever think you see a shadow in the corner of your eye and look up and no one is there? Your eyes are not playing tricks on you. What you are seeing is the phenomenon of ghostly figurations that are still lingering. By practicing these eye exercises you will be able to fully comprehend or see psychic energy not only from those around you and living, but also from those who have passed on and never left due to an attachment of some kind. Here is a good practice chart for you to begin with.

EXERCISE 10
The Spiral Chart

This chart helps strengthen depth vision and the muscles of the iris and helps keep both eyes working together. You see most things through both eyes. When you look at an object, both eyes are focused on it. When you change your gaze from something near to something far or vice versa, the muscles in your eye change the shape of the lens so that the new object of attention will come into focus on the retina. As you get older it is more difficult for your eyes to make this shift from far to near. It doesn't have to be this way.

This is the kind of exercise that developmental optometrists give their clients who are dyslexics, athletes, poor readers, and ordinary people who are not functioning to their full potential visually.

1. Look at the chart (Figure 3) and draw your focus out of that spiraling tunnel as if pulling the innermost point outward.

2. Then shift, allowing your eyes to be drawn into the center of the chart.

3. Shift slowly in and out, in and out, in and out. Mentally see it as if you were pulling the spiral toward you and

Figure 3. Spiral Chart for Exercise #10

then sending it away from you. It will begin to take on a three-dimensional form.

4. If you are having difficulty seeing the spiral three-di-mensionally, focus your eyes on the outer edge of the spiral and follow it around and around until you arrive in the center. Then reverse the direction and allow yourself to come out of the spiral. Usually by the second or third time you will begin to experience the in-and-out, three-dimensional effect.

5. Perform this exercise for no more than three or four minutes. You will feel the inner eye muscles working throughout this exercise. If your eyes begin to hurt or strain, stop immediately.

EXERCISE 11
Circle of Arrows Chart

1. This exercise works your eyes in a similar way as the Spiral Chart exercise. Look at the Arrow Chart (Figure 4). Draw your focus out of the spiraling maze as if pulling the innermost point outward.

2. Shift your direction, allowing your eyes to follow the chart in the opposite direction of movement, switching from clockwise to counterclockwise. Do this slowly at first.

3. See if you can pull the arrows out of sequence, sending them away from you and toward you. They should take on a three-dimensional form.

4. Keep your eyes focused on one section of arrows, either the top section or bottom section. Don't waiver from top to bottom or from side to side.

5. If you are having trouble seeing three-dimensionally, focus your eyes on the outer edge of the chart and follow the arrows around and around. Then, go in the other direction. Usually by the second or third time you do both of these procedures, you will begin to experience the three-dimensional effect—or else you will get a big headache trying. Do it slowly at first to achieve the best results.

Figure 4. Circle of Arrows Chart for Exercise #11

6. Perform this exercise for no more than three or four minutes a day. You will feel your inner muscles working throughout this exercise. If your eyes begin to hurt or strain, stop immediately.

ALTERED STATES OF CONSCIOUSNESS

Using an altered state of consciousness to elicit imagery for creative problem solving is a good application for learning to channel your higher self. To begin with, you should think more about channeling, more intensively than you think about any of the other exercises in this book.

EXERCISE 12
Entering a Trance State to Ponder a Question

1. To enter a trance state, you should be completely alone, with no disturbances. I prefer the comfort of my own bedroom. You may find another room in the house that is more comfortable for you. Or sit outside on warm grass, near some trees. You can also enter this state of mind by being hypnotized.

2. Close your eyes and breathe in and out, focusing your attention on your breathing. If you are breathing fast, try to listen to your heartbeat and think of slowing it down. Breathe slower, slower, slower, until you feel the air within the room and your breathing is at the same rate of speed. When you have accomplished this, you are in a trance mode.

3. Once you have mastered the trance state, allow your mind to run freely. I like to think of running through fields of flowers, with the background of a fluffy-cloud sky, birds chirping, or anything connected to Mother Nature. Be aware of thoughts that may whisper to you.

4. Start asking questions of your thoughts. Allow your mind to run freely.

5. Accept any immediate thoughts or feelings. Be sensitive to the images that arise. Often a solution comes in the dream of a single image rather than all at once. That single image can be the intuition of your higher self speaking in a very succinct manner.

EXERCISE 13
Using a Trance State to Interpret a Dream

1. Enter a trance state.

2. While in this trance state, have a friend read one of your dreams aloud to you.

3. Then, call upon the highest energy within you and allow yourself to speak about the dream.

I have found that even amateurs can deliver quite a meaningful discourse about their own dreams in this manner. Deep within all of us we know the truth about ourselves. If we are willing to assume the responsibility for consciously knowing the truth, we can use this method to bring that knowledge into awareness. For this purpose, the trance state itself may prove to be less important than an attitude of acceptance.

Have you ever wanted to send a telepathic message to someone to seek assistance? The early research I reviewed on hypnosis at a distance suggests that possibility. Psychics have admitted to this ability, but have been loath to use it. We will talk more about telepathy later.

These kinds of methods are explored more fully in chapter 4, "Intuition and Your Personal Patterns."

SEEING YOUR OWN ENERGY FIELD

What exactly are the best conditions for seeing psychic energy? This is an area of study that holds a lot of disagreement. Some say it is easier in the dark because the subtle lights will stand out more. Unfortunately, the light energy given off by the body (biophoton radiation) is absorbed by the darkness. On the other hand, darkness forces the rods of the eye to work extra hard to give you "night vision." Others say that seeing psychic energy is best in a brightly lit area, as the light spectrum has freer play and greater activity. In bright lights the eye cones (the refraction of light behind the retina) are excited and higher intensities and subtle colors are more easily detected. This is truer for young adults because there is greater activation of energy behind the base of the brain than in an older person.

I have found that there is a middle ground for seeing your psychic energy more freely. Initially it is most effective if you use a dimly lit room. You want to physically see your energy field first. As you develop the ability to detect it, then you can more easily fine-tune it to determine the colors. So, for the beginner, I recommend starting with the dimly lit environment. A room at dusk is an excellent time and place to experiment. Dim light forces you to activate your night vision. It forces the rods to absorb and register more of the light spectrum, especially at levels not ordinarily apparent.

EXERCISE 14
Hand Exercise

1. You will need a dim light, a plain white wall, and a piece of plain white cardboard. (It must be large enough to allow your hand to stand out against it).

2. Take time to relax before performing this exercise. If you have been using the eye-chart exercise, you may want to do an abbreviated version as a warm-up.

3. Extend one of your hands out in front of you twelve to eighteen inches. With your other hand, hold the plain white cardboard behind it. Your hand will stand out against the white surface.

4. With your hand flattened and suspended above the white cardboard, the light emanations will be more easily detected as you softly focus your eyes upon it. At first a soft haze will appear. If you have been practicing, the haze will reflect colors as well.

5. With your hands about three inches apart in front of you, begin your focusing. Concentrate first at the top edges of your hands and then soft-focus upon the entire area around them. Allow the soft gaze to look between and around. I can't emphasize enough that you have to concentrate. The energy of your hands will begin to stand out.

6. Next, with your hand flattened on the white cardboard, focus your attention upon the tips of your fingers. Hold this focus for about thirty seconds.

7. Now shift your gaze from the tips of your fingers to take in your entire hand and the cardboard. Relax your eyes. As you move from a pinpointed focus to a general focus, you will begin to detect a soft haze outlining the shape of your hand against the cardboard.

8. If you have difficulty with this, perform some of the eye exercises with your hand against the cardboard. Focus in and out. Move your eyes around the edge of your hand. Shift from the concentrated focus to the soft focus. If you have been practicing, the haze will appear. You can do this with other objects. I have found that by following the base of a tree to the top on a hot, sunny day, I can see the energy level of that tree. What is totally amazing is that if you are in an environment with many trees, for instance on a mountaintop, you can actually see the energy level of all of the trees against the backdrop of the sky.

9. Pay attention to any colors you may detect as well, even if they are fleeting. You may see hints of colors or flashes, and there is often a tendency to discount them. Don't!

10. The next step is to use both hands. Extend them both out in front of you, palms facing toward you. They should be eye level and about three to four inches apart. There should be a blank wall behind them.

11. What you actually see may vary. There may be a soft haze that surrounds your hands. There may be flashes of color or a steady color. You may see something like a heat wave rising up off the street on a hot summer day. In the beginning, it is almost always a pale white or blue, almost colorless. As you develop your ability, the color and its intensity as well as vibrations will become more discernible to your naked eye.

SEEING THE PSYCHIC ENERGY OF OTHERS

The next step is to begin working to see the psychic energy levels of others. If you have been doing the exercises in this book, you should be able to start experiencing significant results within a month or two. It depends on your consistency of practice and your persistence.

ADVANCED EXERCISE 15
Circling the Forehead—
Working with Another Person's Field

1. Have your partner stand flat against a blank white wall. Using a dimly lit room is most effective in the beginning.

2. Stand or sit eight to ten feet away. You must be able to see your partner from head to toe as well as a large surrounding blank area.

3. Begin by focusing your line of sight at the forehead of your partner. From the forehead, circle the eyes around

the body of your partner in a clockwise direction. Do this as quickly as possible, making several revolutions. At this point, you are simply exciting the cones and rods of the eyes.

4. Return your focus to the forehead or to the top of the head. Hold a concentrated focus on this point for fifteen to thirty seconds.

5. Shift from a concentrated focus to a soft one that encompasses a wide area around the body. Hold this soft focus, passively observing. The psychic energy field of the head and shoulders usually stands out most strongly.

6. Repeat the whole procedure as necessary. You are beginning to see the psychic energy of others!

THE MEANING OF COLORS
IN THE HUMAN ENERGY FIELD
Language, Color, Mood, Health

Color is an intimate part of our lives. It affects us all, and it reflects us all. It is used to describe our physical health, our moods, our attitudes, and even our spiritual experiences. Listen to people speak and notice how often color is used as part of their descriptive vocabulary.

"I'm in the pink today."

"He was so angry, he turned red."

"She was feeling a little blue."

"They are just green with envy."

"It was one of those golden experiences."

"I hope you never turn the color of this page."

Color is a property of light. When light is broken down into different wavelengths, we end up with different colors. Hold a prism up to the sunlight; it will display a rainbow on an opposite surface. Those seven colors of the rainbow are only a small fraction of the light spectrum. There are a multitude of shades and variances of each color.

The energy of your own psyche reflects itself in light and color. The color, its clarity, and its location all indicate different things about someone's physical, emotional, and mental as well as spiritual being. As you work with the exercises in this book, you will begin to visually detect the colors of your field. Until then, you can use dowsing rods or pendulums to help you identify the colors of your energy field. Determining the colors is the easy part. The difficult part is understanding and interpreting those colors.

We are all sensitive to color. We are also sensitive to what it may reflect. We may not have given much attention to the spectrum of colors or to what colors we wear. We have all had experiences where we wondered about a friend because her "color" was a bit off. We have also heard comments about how the color of a blouse or shirt is either wonderful for someone or washes out or drains the person's personality. Many times these comments reflect unconscious impressions of psychic energy fields.

Different colors reflect different attitudes, moods, and energy patterns. Although you can identify generally what certain colors reflect, you must keep in mind the multitude of shades within a particular color's spectrum.

Guidelines for Seeing Colors

There are many shades of yellow, green, etc. Understanding the significance of those shades takes time and practice. In determining what colors are within your energy field, there are certain guidelines to keep in mind.

Those colors closest to the physical body usually reflect physical conditions and energies. The outer colors reflect emotional, mental, and spiritual energies.

The clearer and more pastel the colors, the better. Muddier and denser colors can reflect imbalances, overactivity, and other problems in the area to which the colors are connected.

Dark colors that are also bright can indicate high energy levels. This is not necessarily negative. You do not want to jump to any conclusions. There is often more than one color in a psychic energy field for each individual. Each color will reflect different aspects. You must learn how these different colors interact and the effect that combination can have. Again, that takes time and practice.

Interpretation Is Another Matter

When you start to see other people's energy fields, keep in mind that you are looking at them through your own energy level. To interpret what you are seeing, you need to be aware of this. The eye exercises can assist you in seeing your own energy level in a mirror. If your energy level is predominately yellow and the other person's is blue, you may actually see green. Often the subconscious mind is aware of this and makes that adjustment naturally, but you must be careful about jumping to conclusions.

It is important not to make judgments of people based on what you see in their energy fields. What you see and how you interpret it depends a great deal on your own state of mind at the time. Consider the pros and cons of what is associated with that color, along with specific areas to which it is connected. You do not have the right to tell someone else what to do. Bring up the observations, explain possible significances, and then let the other person make her own decisions and choices.

Learn to use your own intuition in interpreting. Ask questions about what you are observing and what you think it may relate to. Only in this way, through the other person's feedback, can you develop the standard for your interpretations. Remember that the color, the location, and the clarity can all indicate different things. Your task is to learn to synthesize them.

Energy levels change frequently. The colors closest to the body can go through many changes in a single day. Every strong emotion and every strong physical or mental activity can result in color and light fluctuations. Do you remember the mood ring? When placed on a finger, it would change colors—red for an excited person, black for a person who is cold and has no activity, etc. Colors are related to the energy level and the strong emotions attached to it.

Our psychic energies change all throughout our life. As you develop the ability to see the colors of your energy levels, you will find that an individual has a predominant color or colors that remain with them forever.

Usually when learning, the first colors to appear are shades of gray and light blue. Do not become discouraged. However, if the colors do not become readily apparent, keep up with your eye exercises. As you work with the exercises, all of this will change. Do not become discouraged if it seems like it is taking forever. Sometimes when you place your thoughts on other things, like the sensitivity to hearing that still small voice within you, the colors of the psychic energy field will automatically pop up just when you aren't paying attention.

As you begin to develop the ability to see your own psychic energy field, you will also see that of others, and you will also notice little things that we often take for granted, such as the energy fields of trees, animals, and children. Many times an elderly person will not have any color in the energy field. When you see no color at all this means that his or her time is almost up here on earth. Also, some adults receive energy from little children. How much energy a child has! As grandparents we (without knowing it) actually draw into our own energy field the energy of our grandchildren. That is what makes us feel so young when we are with them. We are renewed. For the same reason, we want to stay away from black or dull gray energy fields, especially if our own energy is not strong.

Some colors can be destructive; they can stimulate or depress, repel or attract. Colors can even attract males and females. Colors can reflect the positive and the negative, and when perceived within the psychic energy field, they provide a key to the personality, moods, maturity, and health of that individual.

It takes a great deal of practice to interpret the color shades seen within a psychic energy field. Each color has its own characteristic, but each shade of that color changes that characteristic a little.

This book is not intended to provide all of the nuances of color interpretation within an energy field. The colors closest to the body reflect aspects of an individual's physical condition and also those energies present in their lives. The colors and energies further away from the body often indicate the energy will also be moving within that person's life. With practice you will be able to determine the time elements of certain energy patterns by the color and the location of the color with respect to the physical body.

THE MEANINGS OF EACH COLOR
Red

Red is the color of strong energy, fire, and primal creative force. It is the life-promoting energy. Red is hot. It indicates strong passion, mind, and will. This dynamic color reflects anger, love, hate, and unexpected changes. It can indicate new birth and transmutation. Red affects the circulatory system and the reproductive system (sexual energy), and it awakens latent abilities and talents. Too much red or muddiness can reflect overstimulation, inflammation, or imbalance. It may reflect nervousness, temper, aggression, impulsivity, or excitement.

Orange

Orange is the color of warmth, creativity, and emotions. It is an indication of courage, joy, and sociability. Orange reflects an opening of new awareness—especially of the subtle realms (astral plane) of life.

Yellow

Yellow is one of the first and easiest psychic energy colors to be seen. Pale yellow around the hairline can indicate optimism. Yellow is the color of mental activity and sunshine. It can signify new learning opportunities, lightness, wisdom, enthusiasm, and spiritual development (especially in the pale yellow to white spectrum). Yellow represents the power of ideas and awakening psychic abilities and clairvoyance. Deeper and muddier shades of yellow indicate excessive thinking and analyzing. It can stand for being overly critical and dogmatic as well as having feelings of being deprived of recognition.

Green

Green is the color of sensitivity and growing compassion. It reflects growth, sympathy, and calm. It indicates a person who is reliable, dependable, and open-minded. Bright greens moving toward the blue spectrum reveal healing ability. Green is the color of abundance, strength, and friendliness. The muddier or darker shades can reflect uncertainty and miserliness. The muddier shades often reflect jealousy and possessiveness as well. Green also indicates self-doubt and mistrust.

Blue

Next to yellow, *blue* is one of the easiest colors to see in the psychic energy field. It is the color of calm and quietness. It reflects devotion, truth, and seriousness. Blue indicates an ability for clairaudience and telepathy. The lighter shades of blue reflect an active imagination and good intuition. The deeper shades signify a sense of loneliness, which on one level points to a lifelong quest for the Divine. The deep blues express levels of devotion. Royal blue shades indicate honesty and good judgment. They can also indicate the person has found or is about to find his chosen work. The muddier shades of blue reflect blocked perceptions, melancholy, worry, domination, fearfulness, forgetfulness, and oversensitivity.

Violet (or Purple)

Violet (or purple) is the color of warmth and transmutation. It is the color for the blending of the heart and the mind, the physical with the spiritual. Violet reflects independence and intuition, as well as dynamic and important dream activity. It can indicate someone who is searching. These purple shades often reflect an ability to handle affairs with practicality and worldliness. The paler shades of violet and purple indicate humility and spirituality. Red-purple signifies great passion or strength of will. It may also reflect a need for greater individual effort. The darker and muddier shades of violet can suggest a need to overcome something. They can reflect intense erotic imaginations as well. Tendencies to be overbearing, need sympathy, and feel misunderstood are also seen in muddier shades.

Pink

Pink is the color of compassion, love, and purity. It can reflect joy and comfort and a strong sense of companionship. When seen in the psychic energy field it can indicate the quiet, modest type of individual who has a love of art and beauty. The muddier shades of pink can suggest immaturity. Pink can reveal truthfulness or a lack of it. It can also reflect times of new love and a new vision.

Gold

Gold expresses dynamic spiritual energy and a true coming into one's own power. It indicates the higher energies of devotion and a restoration of harmony. Gold suggests strong enthusiasm and great inspiration. It also points to a time of revitalizing. For instance, there were times when I desperately wanted something to happen. It was like a wish I had made and wanted to come true. So, concentrating on what I wanted, I immediately looked toward the divine heavens and imagined gold sparkles illuminating my thoughts. These gold sparkles, which are very strong in energy, made my dream come true. This can also happen when you do a healing. Muddier shades of gold can indicate the person is still in the process of awakening higher inspiration and has not yet clarified it within his life. Gold reflects the alchemical process is still active, that is, the person is still working to turn the lead of life into gold.

White

White is often seen in the psychic energy field prior to any actual colors. It is sometimes perceived as a diaphanous shade. White has all colors within it, and when it does appear strongly within the energy field it can be in conjunction with other colors. This is how you can know whether it is an actual energy color or just a poor perception of the psychic energy field. When the white does stand out as a color in the energy field, it reflects truth and purity and indicates that the energy of the individual is cleansing and purifying itself. This color often reveals an awakening of greater creativity as well. When you have this kind of energy it is important to protect yourself.

Gray

Gray is a color of initiation. It can indicate a movement toward unveiling innate abilities. Those shades of gray that lean toward silver reflect an awakening of the feminine energies. These are the energies and abilities of illumination, intuition, and creative imagination. The darker shades of gray express physical imbalances, especially if seen next to specific areas of the physical body. They can also indicate a need to leave no task undone. Many grays in the energy field of the psyche can signify a person who is secretive and the lone-wolf type.

Brown

Brown often appears in the psychic energy field. Although many people think of it as reflecting a lack of energy or an imbalance, this is not always so. Brown is the color of the earth. When it shows itself in the psychic energy field, especially in the areas above the head and around the feet, brown can reflect new growth. It indicates establishing new roots and a desire to accomplish. Brown stands for industry and organization. On the other hand, brown across the face or touching the head may indicate a lack of and need for discrimination. If seen in the psychic energy field of the chakras, it can indicate that those centers need to be cleaned because of a clogging of their energies. Brown is often difficult to interpret as it can easily reflect physical problem areas, but you must be careful about jumping to conclusions when you see it. Information from the individual being observed is the best means of understanding what you are really seeing.

Black

Black is one of the most confusing colors in the psychic energy spectrum. I have heard individuals say that when black shows up in the energy field, it is an indication of death or a terrible disease. I have *not* found that to be true. I just sense a strong, sad feeling from the other person's energy field and almost borrow their energy as they submit their energy to mine. If they have a crisis, I can feel it, and that is when I tell them something in their life is awry. Or I can sense sadness. I can do this in a practical way, and you can, too. Black is also a color of protection. It is a color that can shield an individual from outside energies. When seen in an energy field it indicates that person is protecting himself. It can also indicate that he has a lot of secrets. There is nothing necessarily wrong with that as long as it is not taken to the extremes. Black can also signify a new understanding of burdens and sacrifices. It can reflect imbalances. Physical imbalances often show up as black or darkened areas in the energy field around the physical body. The location provides clues. In the outer edges of the energy field black indicate holes in the energy field. I have seen this in the energy levels of those who were victims of child abuse or domestic violence and those who are or were strong substance abusers (alcohol, drugs, tobacco, etc.). Schizophrenics have huge holes in their energy fields or hardly any field at all. This is also true for people with brain damage and developmental problems.

Silver Twinklies

Another aspect that I have observed should be mentioned. I have often seen within the energy field what looks like soft, twinkling lights. They are usually sparkly and silvery, and I have found that they may indicate several things. These *"twinklies"* are almost always a great sign of creativity and fertility. When they appear within the energy field, greater activity is being generated within the individual's life. I have seen these most frequently around women or teenage girls—more so than in boys. When I do see them around a woman whose energy field I am reading, I will ask her if she is pregnant. These twinklies are always present around pregnant women and women who have delivered a child within the past six to nine months.

My own theory is that these twinklies indicate the activation of creativity and fertility within the individual's life. Creativity and fertility can take a number of forms. My theory is that when this creativity becomes so active that it shows up as lights in the psychic energy field, it draws new souls close to that individual. Then, if the opportunity arises, as in pregnancy, the new souls simply "slip in." If the person I am reading is not pregnant, I will let her know that there is a great likelihood for pregnancy to occur in the next six to nine months.

If the fertility does not culminate with a physical pregnancy, then it will play itself out in another area of the individual's life. Usually within six months, ten at the most, something will be born into that person's life that ultimately will be as life changing as a new child. A positive, beneficial door will open. Although it may take as long as six months for this creative opportunity to come to fruition, it is usually dynamic and positive.

As you develop your psychic energy sight, you will become aware of the subtle differences in colors. A study of chromotherapy and color will assist you in not only becoming more sensitive to it, but also in understanding the significance of color.

CONCLUSION

The above modalities seem different from each other because humans are unique in their abilities and in what inspires them. Our creativity in garnering aids could be much more developed if we simply relearned what we knew about psychic abilities through the past ages.

We are born with a specific biological link to the psychic realm. The universal knowledge is there waiting for us to tap into it. You have to trust in your feelings and have reverence for the courage to act on what is right for you. Read this book and learn how to trust your own psychic intuition and inner voice. All the issues of intuition and inner knowing are particularly connected to your psychic energy center because it is with your sixth sense that you awaken your awareness, evoking a broader and more continuous participation in these abilities. Is it chance? No. It is beyond chance that events happen that cannot be explained. Inner knowledge embraces all aspects of life in a balanced manner. This inner knowing, intuition, and consciousness awareness are the seeds of manifestation.

The Sanskrit word for the psychic energy within us is *ajna,* which means "command and control." But the process of opening to more knowledge about the psychic abilities within you cannot be controlled with ordinary ego or by collecting, hoarding, and manipulating information. Instead, look at it as a form of gradual surrender to knowledge that is already there. Because intuition is already available, the only thing you need to do in order to unlock your psychic abilities is to feel your resistance and desire and gracefully accept it because this ability is already there for you. With this inherent ability that is your birthright, you can enjoy abundance by stretching and transcending the limits of what you have been programmed to conceive as real.

🖐

Your Psychic Center

There is an ancient system of development known as the mystical Qabala. It employs sound, visualization, and breathing to pump up your psychic energy with tremendous amounts of energy, almost like working out.

This system of development helps seal leaks and holes within your energy field. It stabilizes and balances your psyche and increases your energy levels so that you have greater amounts with which to carry out your daily tasks. It prevents your energies from being overtapped.

Performing exercises simply to vibrate the energies within your psyche is important for many reasons. Discipline your activities to include determination in cleansing not only your psyche but also your body from all outward invasions from negative sources. It is significant to ground your energies by performing a few exercises so that no harm or drainage from others can leave your psychic centers empty. The more psychic energy you have, the more you will be able to perceive things not seen clearly in everyday life. I am reminded of a pile of sand. Every time a grain of sand is taken away or destroyed, the pile gets smaller and smaller. If you don't return what you borrowed the pile will shrink until there is nothing left. You can see why it is important to return energy to its rightful place by building and storing as much as possible. The end result is protective and strengthening.

The following is a simple grounding exercise to perform whenever you feel unbalanced.

EXERCISE 16
Basic Grounding Exercise

1. This exercise uses ancient Hebrew names for God-like mantras in conjunction with specific images and breathing. This combination creates what is called a synergistic effect, making the result eight times as strong. The three aspects—naming, imagining, and breathing—increase the energy exponentially.

2. Stand with toes curled under. Don't let your arches roll outward or inward but keep them straight. Relax the knees, keep the back straight, and pull the perineum down toward the earth, imagining that gravity has become stronger. Breathe all the way up the back into the head and make sure the breath comes down through the face, neck, and chest to the gut and out through the earth. Keep doing it until you feel energy moving down and out through your toes.

3. Visualize a crystalline white sphere of light gently coming toward you from the heavens until it is just over your head. It is vibrant and alive with energy. As you vibrate the name see and feel this light growing with intensity and filling your body.

4. Softly sound the name EHEIEHUH (Eh-huh-yeh). Emphasize each syllable, feeling the crown of your head come alive with energy. Repeat this name five to ten times. This name translates as, *"I am that I am."*

5. Pause and visualize a shaft of light descending from this sphere, pouring down toward your throat where a second sphere of light forms. As you vibrate aloud the God-name YHVH ELOHIM (Yah-hoh-vah-eh-loh-heem), this sphere of light grows more vibrant and brilliant. Vibrate this name five to ten times. This name means, *"The Lord God of Creation."*

6. Pause and visualize a shaft of light descending from this sphere down to the heart area of the body. Here a third sphere of brilliant light forms. Slowly, syllable by syllable, vibrate the name YHVH ELOAH VADAATH (Yah-hoh-vah-eh-loh-ah-vuh-dahth). Repeat this five to ten times, feeling the sphere of light grow stronger and filling that part of your body. This name means, *"God made manifest in the mind."*

7. Pause and visualize a shaft of light descending from this sphere of light down to the area of your groin. See and feel a fourth sphere of light form with brilliance. Vibrate

the name SHADDAI EL CHAI (Shad-dye-el-keye) slowly five to ten times. Feel the energy coming alive in this part of the body. This name means, *"The Almighty Living God."*

8. Pause and visualize the shaft of light descending from this fourth sphere of light down to the area of your feet. Here a fifth sphere forms, while the shaft descends down into the heart of the earth itself. As you vibrate the sound of the God-name ADONAI HAARETZ HEH (Ah-doh-nye-hah-ah-retz-hey), the sphere grows with crystalline brilliance. Repeat this five to ten times. This name means, *"Lord of the Earth."*

   You now have formed a balance through your entire body and psychic centers. Bring your attention back to the top or crown of your head and begin rhythmic breathing. As you exhale slowly to a count of four, see and feel your energy pour down the left side of your body, radiating outward, strengthening your psychic energy field on that side of your body. Inhale for a count of four and draw energy up the right side of your body from your feet to the crown of your head. See and feel this energy radiating outward, strengthening your energy field on that side of your body. Hold your breath for a count of four, and then repeat the exhalation and inhalation. Do this four or five times.

9. Now, as you exhale, see and feel the energy stream down the front of your body for a count of four. Inhale,

and allow it to stream up the back. Hold for a count of four and repeat four or five times. You have now strengthened your entire psychic energy field. Feel this energy surrounding you. Know that it has sealed up any leaks. Know that it has replaced any lost energy.

10. Now feel the energy gathering at your feet. As you inhale, draw rainbow-colored light up through your feet, up through the middle pillar to the top of your head. As you exhale, spray that rainbow light out the top of your head to fill up your entire psychic energy field with its color and energy. Pause and allow yourself to bask in this brilliant and renewed energy field.

This exercise cleanses the entire energy field, like doing a scan disk and defragmentation on your computer. It strengthens and facilitates the development of higher energies, including your own psychic abilities. Because it raises the energy of the individual to such a high level, it also helps in the development of vision of the energy field. It increases overall perception and sensitivity—physical and otherwise.

I teach this exercise in my workshops and stress it as absolutely fundamental. It should be employed by anyone wishing to open up higher faculties. It is so powerful and effective that it should become the staple of those just beginning as well as those who have been involved in the metaphysical for a long time. It is grounding, protective, and strengthening.

A dynamic variation to this Qabala exercise is to incorporate a sixth sphere of light. This sixth sphere is activated in the area of the third eye or brow center. This main center is linked to physical vision as well as psychic vision (clairvoyance). This particular variation is even more dynamic in stimulating auric vision, or the ability to see the psychic haze emitted from your energy field.

EXERCISE 17

Variation on the Basic Grounding Exercise: The Qabala of Light

1. Sit in a relaxed state of mind. Close your eyes. You may listen to soft, comforting music if you wish.

2. Visualize a crystalline ball of light descending from the heavens to come and rest at the top of your head. As you vibrate the name EHEIEHUH (Eh-huh-yeh), feel the crown of your head come alive with energy. It tingles and your scalp may feel itchy. If so, you know the exercise is working.

3. Visualize a shaft of light descending from this sphere to form a second sphere in the area of your brow, or third eye. Intone the name JEHOVAH (Yah-hoh-vah) softly. Visualize the sound carrying to the ends of the universe and back. Oh, what a beautiful name. It raises goosebumps on my arms. Feel your inner eyes coming alive with energy. Repeat this sound five to ten times.

4. From this sphere, the shaft of light descends further to form a third sphere of light in the area of your throat. Vibrate the God-name JEHOVAH ELOHIM (Yah-hoh-vah-eh-loh-heem). See and feel this sphere of light come to life with brilliant vibrancy. Your throat will feel scratchy as if you have a sore throat; swallow hard and then repeat this exercise five to ten times.

5. From this sphere, the shaft descends and forms a fourth sphere of light in the area of your heart. It comes alive with each intonation of the name JEHOVAH ELOAH VADAATH (Yah-hoh-vah-eh-loh-ah-vuh-daath). Repeat five to ten times.

6. Pause and visualize the shaft of light descending from the heart sphere to the area of your groin. There, a fifth sphere of light forms. See it form and radiate brilliance with each intonation of the name SHADDAI EL CHAI (Shah-dyc-cl-keye).

7. Again pause, and then visualize the shaft of light descending from this fifth sphere to your feet. Here a sixth sphere of light forms, and the shaft continues down into the heart of the planet. As you intone the name ADONAI HAARETZ HEH (Ah-doh-nye-hah-retz-hey), see the sixth sphere of light coming to life for you.

You have now performed the Qabala of Light exercise. You have activated the inner centers of light that will strengthen and protect your energy field and help reawaken your inner psyche. Now do the rhythmic breathing and visualization techniques in the previous exercise. Give thanks for this wonderful celebration of renewed extrasensory understanding.

HOW ENERGY FLOWS

The chakras are subtle energy centers in the human being. The term chakra is Sanskrit for "circle" or "wheel." The chakras have been known in traditional Asian medicine for thousands of years and are used for diagnosis as well as for treating disorders on physical, emotional, and mental levels. They have a variety of functions. On one hand, they are the subtle counterpart of the material organs or groups of organs associated with them. On the other hand, they determine how our existence develops on the different planes of being, thus reflecting our respective states of evolution.

The Opening of the Chakras

If you can accept your chakras in all the realms and live out their energies with pleasure, you are very close to enlightenment. This means that you are in close contact with the universal spirit that takes everything as it is, loving everything and containing everything.

If you want to grow toward higher awareness and a greater capacity for love, look to nature as a good example of how the principle of the chakra system works.

The root chakra is very low in the trunk, between the legs, whereas the sexual chakra is found right above the pubic bone. Both of these centers belong to the earth realm.

The following classification needs a brief explanation. There are six chakras I work with and ten important minor chakras. Although there are many more, these ten are quite sufficient in most instances when channeling your energy. I use the following terms for the six major chakras:

First chakra = root chakra

Second chakra = sexual chakra

Third chakra = personality chakra

Fourth chakra = heart chakra

Fifth chakra = expressive chakra

Sixth chakra = knowledge chakra

The ten minor chakras are located as follows:

Two minor chakras in the palms control contact with the environment and the transfer of life energy. On an energy level they are connected with the kidneys and with the second, third, and fourth major chakras.

Two minor chakras in the arches of the feet control contact with the earth, reception of energy (grounding), and the delivery of "subtle garbage" back to the earth. On an energy level they are connected with the first and third major chakras and with the psychic energy level.

Two minor chakras just below both the shoulders control our way of handling responsibility. On an energy level they are connected with the third and fifth major chakras.

Two minor chakras in the knee joints control flexibility as well as the ability to teach and learn. Flexibility includes the faculty of creating varying energy potentials and gradients that make teaching and learning possible in the first place. Furthermore, pride and feelings of inferiority come in here. On an energy level these chakras are connected with the fifth and sixth major chakras.

Two minor chakras in the elbow joints control our ability to give and accept and our power of self-assertion. Energetically, they are connected with the lungs, the pancreas, and the second and third major chakras.

The seventh chakra, also called the crown chakra, develops through the purification of the other six energy centers. Basically, the seventh chakra can only be understood by following the exercises listed in this book for full capacity of your psychic energy levels.

Balancing the Channels

The energy channels in the body are considered to exist on the etheric level, which is a kind of double of the physical level that surrounds the body. One of the ways to keep this etheric level balanced in its energies is to do the circle exercise daily. See Figure 4, The Circle of Arrows.

REMEMBER THE
LARGER CONNECTION

There are many paths to the soul, and we can develop our psychic awareness in the context of spiritual growth. We will talk more about spiritual matters in chapter 9, "Spiritual Dimensions." One path in learning to develop your psychic ability occurs with the help of a loving, supportive family and friends who give honest feedback.

Another path is regular meditation or prayer, which allow the mind and body to be one and therefore to be more receptive to the soul's vibrations. Attention to God, helping others, and supporting the talents in others that emerge in the form of psychic abilities, all contribute to our own development.

CROSS-CULTURAL CONNECTIONS: THE UNIVERSAL NATURE

We have five senses: hearing, smell, sight, taste, and touch. Buddhists, however, are conscious of and sensitive to a sixth sense. They call it the phenomena sense. It is about awareness and consciousness, and we can develop it.

There have always been people in all cultures who have special access to the universe and perform this function for the whole group. These are witches, healers, philosophers, shamans, priestesses, drum dancers, etc. Everyone longs to be in touch with "the other world." Of course that world is right here, in another dimension. All cultures wish for some members of their group to develop their psychic abilities for the benefit of all.

LISTENING TO YOUR BODY

We are in the midst of a revolution. It is occurring in one of the most established, conservative enterprises in the

Western world—the field of medicine—and will have a pro-found impact on how we view the world and how we live in it. This revolution, slow to gain adherents, is the knowl-edge of how the mind affects the body.

There is a general notion that when a person is ill he needs to be considerate when thinking about his health. For example, if a body part is not functioning properly, thinking positively is part of the healing process.

In order to develop our psychic abilities further, we sim-ply must learn to tune into the vibrations and to set aside the conscious mind and the significance of the body. The body is a temple where we encounter psychic energies. We can think of our body as an instrument of psychic conduit energies, someplace for our inner soul to plug in as if we were to plug an appliance into a socket. Although our psy-chic abilities are like lovely music, they resonate with vi-brations in a less than perfect manner and this distorts the music, or our psychic abilities. Psychic energies are of the soul, but the soul finds itself projected into the earth where the soul expresses itself through the vehicle of the body. Thus we must examine the body of our psychic abili-ties fully.

HOW THE BODY/MIND RELATIONSHIP AFFECTS PSYCHIC AWARENESS

The impact of our emotional state is crucial to bodily func-tioning and our health. Attitudes are chronic or stable emotional frames of the mind. Together, our emotions and attitudes are like drugs in our body.

Our attitudes and emotions can poison us or make us "high." The discovery of the brain's production of endorphins, natural euphoriants, has led to a number of additional discoveries that vigorous exercise and emotional responses such as being in love can stimulate the production of endorphins. Endorphins and other emotionally triggered chemicals have an effect on the endocrine system and thus on psychic energies within our energy field or aura.

Language

Our language, for instance, has long reflected this secret understanding of the relationship between emotions and bodily processes. We can say that someone's behavior "disgusts" us, as if we knew that the effect of our emotional reaction was to increase a poisonous secretion in our stomachs. When we say, "I can't stomach that," we express our knowledge that our emotional reaction is upsetting the digestive system. The language of emotions is full of such phrases that implicate our bodies. When a person is in a chronic state of emotional arousal—lonely, depressed, or resentful—the chemical effect will begin to cause physical deterioration. Ulcers, headaches, psoriasis, colitis, even allergies and cancer—these are but a few of the syndromes that have come to populate the developing field of "psychosomatic" medicine that many psychics previsioned.

Imagery

One way to communicate with the subconscious mind and the emotional body is through imagery. Dramatic effects are attributed to imagery and have been measured in the immune system. Through imagery, the mind can achieve effective control over the functioning of the cells in the immune system. The creative power of the imagination to pattern physical manifestations is confirmed in the kind of bodily control that can be achieved through imagery. For example, religious statues in churches can have an effect on our perception of our health, as can stones or a rosary. With regard to psychic centers, it is understandable that I stress using visualization with extreme care, for the psychic centers need to be opened in a harmonious pattern.

An Inner Calling to Change

In order to have an attitude change that will drastically shift the way your body feels, you need to get in touch with the beliefs that separate you from this aspect of yourself. You have to become very clear about what has prevented you from continually abiding in this fundamental state of being, which is your birthright. You need to answer questions such as, "Why do I often do the opposite of what I originally set out to do?" Or, "How does my desire for one particular thing ensure what will actually happen."

Our judgments, beliefs, and defense mechanisms set up the very walls that keep us from enjoying true harmony with our psychic self. There is no need to despair, however, because what is there is there for a reason. At a point in our development, as in childhood or adolescence, we needed those same judgments and beliefs in order to survive. But now they keep our sixth sensory perceptor in its place. Whenever our inner call becomes strong enough, however, we have the ability to clear away all obstacles to use our innate abilities. We are not condemned to restrictions in our lives forever. We can look at them as temporary learning tools. What we can always do is cultivate the attitude of gratitude with full-bodied enthusiasm.

EXERCISE 18
Making an Immediate Attitude Change

1. Sit in a comfortable position, your spine erect yet relaxed, your ears over your shoulders, and your shoulders over your hips. Do this for five minutes and feel all of your resistance (in energy) that you have blocked for years flow through your chakra channels. Experience fully with complete enthusiasm all of your negative thoughts, whatever they may be. Recall incidents when your negative beliefs were proved "true," and feel your resulting emotions, which you may feel in your entire body. These emotions will expand and then dissipate.

2. Now I want you to sit cross-legged. Your spine is erect and your forehead is facing upward toward the ceiling or sky. This is best done outside where the energy will

work positively. With your eyes closed, focus any thoughts you have, positive or negative, to the heavens. Try to feel the subtle energies around you. Think of the energy being emitted by the trees, the leaves, the sky, the ground you are sitting on, and the air on your face. After you have felt the energies around you, think about how your body is absorbing them like a sponge. Tell me what happens. Do you feel goosebumps? Does your arm hair stand up? If so, you have achieved positive results and are obtaining outside energies that are not human energy.

3. Feel the warmth of the sun on your face. With eyes closed be thankful for the blessings in your life.

4. After allowing the positive energies to flow through your body, you are ready to experience the kinds of things that do not happen by chance. You will have a more positive outlook; you will be more friendly and helpful. Positivity and gratitude go together and will bring many new experiences you could not have otherwise.

All psychic energy is connected to blockages in the Root Chakra. This energy is located where spirit and matter are linked. The Root Chakra deals with physical manifestations. Located at the lower end of the spine, the Root Chakra's primary function is to manifest the physical expression of universal life force energy. This is the root and support of everything. When the base malfunctions everything malfunctions, as your psychic energy and abilities cannot unfold without support.

We can turn this situation around by simply allowing our true thoughts and emotions to surface by directing all of our attention on them. By acknowledging what we feel and sense we no longer deny the tremendous resistance we have against our psychic energy field. Through our acknowledgement of these same feelings, our resistance dissipates and we are freed from the tendency to struggle over what is real and what is not.

By feeling our energy course through our being, we can accept and neutralize the hooks that bind our consciousness into releasing what is rightfully ours. We can now encompass the heartfelt desires that flow through us in order to gently guide us toward the lessons we came here to learn, at the same time being aware of the danger that if we are not careful, we can begin to overidentify with those lessons.

By energetically feeling these waves of intensity, we can prepare the ground for using our psychic energies to manifest on their own accord. We open ourselves to the wisdom of not striving. We are now able to joyously accept all of what life offers because we can now directly experience our own phenomena that come into being through consciousness of what we really are.

Emotions

What price do we pay for our emotions? How do we clean out our emotional inventory and imbalances regularly?

We all have emotions; some of them are good and some of them aren't. It depends on how you look at them and how you allow them to affect your overall life. Some of us act out; some of us have chronic emotional attitudes that are destructive to others and self-destructive. We can be victims of our own emotional upheavals. Or we can cause turmoil in others with our thoughts, words, and deeds.

Our emotions can kill us. I used to get overexcited about things. I let everything bother me, especially the attitudes of others. I became a people-pleaser. We all need to look at how we deal with our emotions and with various situations.

Emotions flow with the energy inside you. If you have positive energy your emotions will be positive. If you aren't fully charged like a battery with psychic energy, then your daily activities will be affecting only part of you, while the other part is in limbo.

Our emotions show what is inside of us. Orpheus was able to make stones and shrubs weep with his singing. He certainly had a well-functioning Throat Chakra (which is a high energy level). People who have negative energy, like Hitler, are able to persuade people of their own negative worth. So, you become what you preach and you can become what is preached to you.

All of our body's energy centers contain aspects of the other energy centers, and they are all interconnected. One way we promote their harmonious integration is by balancing our emotions, and we do that by setting priorities.

Otherwise we get out of whack easily, experience emotional drainage, and are in constant need of recharging our batteries.

Listen to your emotions. What are they telling you? Do your emotions ignore or overemphasize your daily events? It is always the right time to get back on track. In fact, starting over is something that we do every day. Even though we are always making mistakes (or we wouldn't be alive), we can still help ourselves by learning to control negative energy. We can redirect that energy to more positive outlets. And our positive energy rubs off on those we come into contact with. So what are we waiting for?

Make a daily journal and record what happens when your energy is not up to par and when you feel exuberant and in a positive energy flow. Make sure you write down what happened before your mood changed. Then, ponder all those trivial things you have written down. Chances are it will turn into a mountain of information that you can well use to see what is causing some of your emotions.

Take the time to change your attitude. Yesterday when I went to the grocery store I saw an old woman who couldn't carry a heavy package to her car. So I helped her. Later in the day I was almost hit by a speeding car. I saw the car coming toward me and froze. But somehow I got to the other side of the street before I was hit. I do believe these two incidents are related because of my positive state of mind.

GROOMING THE PSYCHIC CENTERS

It is not necessary to open the psychic centers to manifest psychic abilities. They function as psychic receptors naturally. Psychic functioning is an attribute of healthy, creative functioning that can be cultivated, if one so desires, to include meditation for maximal development. It is always important to cultivate a healthy body, especially if one is to attempt to meditate upon the psychic centers or the energy within.

Good grooming habits for the psychic center will include physical, mental, and emotional as well as spiritual habits, as they all have their effect upon the superconscious mind and its soul body, the endocrine system.

For example, a diet high in vegetables and low in red meat is best suited for someone who wants to excel in psychic abilities. We are what we eat. Recognize this as we incorporate different life forms into our body. Make sure your spinal cord is not blocking the flow of vital energies, and for this I suggest you use the services of a chiropractor or do some stretching exercises to stimulate circulation in your lower back muscles.

A healthy body requires a healthy emotional frame of mind. Fearfulness, chronic anger, depression, and constant stress all have a negative effect at all levels. Dietary factors, such as coffee, sugar, and alcohol, can play a role in worsening the emotional and physical responses to stress. Examine your patterns of thought. Your thinking patterns are favored by spiritual entities such as angels. We can bring more miracles into our lives if we change our thinking patterns.

A person needn't perform spiritual calisthenics in order to develop psychic abilities. Many of the ordinary things that we do and think about have implications for the psychic centers. We can develop a healthy, happy life knowing that by doing so, we are taking care of our physical, emotional, and soul bodies, promoting a natural development of psychic abilities.

HOW TO NURTURE YOUR BODY FOR PSYCHIC WELL-BEING

What do you think about during the day? What do you read? What do you watch on television? What we feed our subconscious through these activities has implications on our psychic center. For example, if you watch a movie on war crimes, it will make your immune system depressed while watching a movie about Christ healing someone strengthens it. In this day and age, when the stresses of life tire us, we get a surge of adrenaline energy from seeing the good guys go after the bad guys, but it is important to remember that psychic development in the context of an overactive solar plexus leads to unwanted psychic effects. It would be better to give the adrenals a rest and to activate the higher centers by watching a restful movie, listening to soothing music, having celestial scents in the room, eating fruit for a snack, and sharing these delights with someone you love. In this pleasurable manner not only can you relax from the cares of the world, but you can also be assured that you are grooming your psychic centers for optimal performance. In such an atmosphere the body of the soul can rekindle its juices and perhaps urge you on to further adventure into developing psychic abilities.

LET YOUR NATURAL ABILITIES EMERGE

I have always liked this next exercise because it deals with finding an area of stress in your life and eliminating it. This is a cruncher and takes a lot of discipline.

EXERCISE 19
Re-energizing Your Center: The Big Cruncher

1. Eliminate television for a week.

2. Turn off the telephone during dinner.

3. Take a walk every day at lunch.

4. Get up every fifteen minutes from your computer, desk, or other work and stretch your arms upward.

5. Lay on the floor every afternoon and stretch your back. You can also do this exercise raising your buttocks off the floor. Hold for a count of ten. Do this lift ten times.

6. Save all your mail until Saturday and do your bills then.

7. After you have done this for one week, you should be able to identify your greatest area of stress. Mine is the telephone. No matter where I am, someone is always calling me. I get away as often as I can to my "abandoned cabin in the wilderness." There is no TV, phone, or mail there. While I have been writing this one para-

graph I have had seventeen telephone calls. You know where I am going this weekend.

8. By identifying just one area where you can reduce your stress, you will make space for yourself and for connections that you want to develop.

PSYCHIC EMERGENCIES

Whenever I do a reading I have people tell me afterward that they have strange experiences such as headaches, flashes of past-life recollections, tremblings, or bizarre psychic experiences.

When we try to develop our psyche in ways other than through the normal realm of meditation and sensitivity, we make ourselves vulnerable to unwanted communication. Sometimes the use of drugs and alcohol can produce "holes" in our energy field that correspond to the vulnerabilities in our etheric body due to the improper functioning of our psychic energy level. These invite invasion from outside influences. It is like opening Pandora's box! When we awaken our psychic energy, it can be quite a roller coaster ride! Imagine the consequences when the energy is reawakened in a haphazard manner.

Such crises exist in great numbers. A weird phenomenon can happen when we least expect it. Anyone who has ever witnessed a person who is going through a spiritual emergency can testify that the opening of the psychic energy field or aura is truly a powerful event. When you work with your psychic energies, do not be tempted to use the full force of what you are developing until you have acquired some skill. Go slowly and have patience. Respect what you have, use it to good purpose, and be good to your body. There are dangers, but use your wisdom and discrimination to attune your energy level in a constructive manner.

EXERCISE 20

General All-purpose Fixer for Psychic Emergencies

1. Listen to the signals from your body. Get away from situations that feel dangerous to you. Cross arms and legs to protect your energy field from being drained if you cannot leave.

2. If you don't want anyone to steal your energy, you should cross your legs or arms. This eliminates the borrower from taking what doesn't rightfully belong to him or her.

3. Focus on what it is you need at the moment to feel better. That focus will eliminate negative energy from entering you and should help you find a way out of the present circumstances.

How to Prevent Psychic Emergencies

The first thing we must do is avoid the situations that put us in jeopardy. We need to be aware that there are many outside forces that can drain us. If you indulge yourself in smoking or drinking alcohol or spend time in the company of people who do, your energy level will decrease. Look at your healthy life as a seesaw. Do you see the negative side of it loaded with weight: gossiping, hurting others, etc.? Do what is right for you. Bring some goodness into your life.

Many serious students should have a teacher/trainer to monitor their growth and to help them stay out of trouble. You may want to have a friend or partner help you. You can write in a journal the day's events, such as gossiping at work and then being splashed by a taxi and your resulting annoyance. Do these things go together, and did expressing your discontent during the day add up to going to bed with a bad attitude? Have a friend help you discuss the negatives you record in your journal for a week. You can see where your energy is going and become more sensitive to what is around you. When you are able to clear out these small negativities, then you will be more sensitive to the big ones and can sense danger for yourself a long way off and into the future. You will take better care of yourself in big ways once you have eliminated the small stuff.

Recently I was in the car with my daughter, who was driving. I suddenly became violently ill. It came over me like a swarm of locusts and was getting worse and worse. I told her to pull over and get out of the car. We got out and I was still ill, barely able to breathe. A tractor-trailer came down the road behind us out of control and barreled into the car ahead of us, crushing it. As soon as the truck was stopped, my violent illness went away. I would never have felt this emergency if I had been filled up with many smaller negativities.

EXERCISE 21

Antidote to a Threatened or Real Emergency

1. *Examine Your State of Mind.* Draw a circle of negative emotions. On the north side is Anger, on the south side is Peacefulness, on the east side put Hostility, and on the west side put Harmony.

2. *Anger and hostility.* See to what degree anger takes up room on your circle. Do you yell at the children? If yes, color one-eighth of the circle red. If you don't, color the left side yellow. Anger is related to heart disease in particular and to a shorter life in general. Angry people also have more accidents. If you are a man, color red next to hostility. Testosterone heightens aggressiveness, argumentation, fighting, and the desire to control. If you are a woman and do not redirect your anger, then you need to put red next to hostility as well.

3. *Depression, sadness, self-pity, hopelessness.* If you are a woman, put green between anger and harmony. The evidence is that depression interferes with recovery from severe illnesses more than it is a cause of disease. For example, in women with breast cancer, the most depressed had fewer natural killer cells. Elderly people who are afraid they won't recover from a fall and are depressed about that possibility tend to be three times

less likely to return to their previous health after they do have a fall. If you are elderly and have health problems, color green between anger and harmony.

4. *Agitation, restlessness, argumentation.* If you argue more than others, try to prove a fact, and tend to think you are never wrong, color red on the circle between the north and east side of the circle. Why do we argue? Is it because of fear or worry? Or is it our ego telling us we are never wrong? Fear and worry tend to have an impact on our immune system. When we are stressed, our T cell and B cell levels drop dramatically. Our energy level is drained, and we tend to catch more colds and flus.

5. *Denial.* Ignorance is an even better word for denial. If you are worried, you will inadvertently do something to physically agitate the situation. When you do this unconsciously you can hurt yourself and others, and your energy is in denial. It's a bit like burning the candle at both ends. People who are "repressors" like this may be more susceptible to diseases like asthma, high blood pressure, and colds. If you feel this tug of war within yourself, then color red between hostility and peacefulness.

6. *The Overall Picture.* Now take a look at the circle. What do you see? Is most of the circle in red? The red areas are where you will want to work for improvement in your overall health. If there is a lot of red on your circle, you need to change your way of thinking. Be more

mindful of what you do, what you say, whom you associate with, what you ingest, your attitude toward others, and your overall attitude. If you have mood swings;
become angry at the drop of a hat; and if anxiety, sadness, or tension come easily, you are twice as likely to
get asthma, chronic headaches, stomach ulcers, heart
disease, or arthritis. If you already have any of these illnesses, color red between the north and south side of
the circle.

In contrast to this, we can look at the following states:

Wholesome energy and health. Consider a state of calm.
You have learned to turn the negative into the positive. You
can turn lemons into lemonade. You have done this in part
with meditation. Through relaxation, you prevent energy
drainage. You are embracing your problems truly, which
enables you to let them go. Letting them go rejuvenates
your energy within. You have obtained a new outlook and
have an explanation for bad things; you don't get depressed and setbacks don't bother you all that much. You
are hopeful about changing situations. Instead of saying
you are stupid when you fail a test, you say it was hard and
next time you will study harder. Positive reasoning adds to
your energy level, excuses do not. Color your circle yellow
when you can reason and embrace your fears.

Confidence. This is a sense of being able to handle a situation knowing that the energy within you will take control
of a specific matter, as all energy is directed like a vein from

a main artery. When you feel this, color yellow between peacefulness and harmony.

Friendliness. This is social connection—how many friends you have or people providing emotional support. These human connections buffer the effects of stress. The group and partners raise the energy level and dissipate negativity, bringing us joy and happiness. Laughing together can be the highest energy and can increase T cells, resulting in the remission of diseases. Joy is the most positive energy, which heals, increases sensitivity, and heightens awareness.

Loving-kindness. This is the best modeling we can send out into the world. And it is the best role model to see for ourselves. You care about people. Your energy starts moving. This strengthens your own energy level and your immune system. Color the circle yellow for the loving-kindness that you show others. Make it part of your everyday life to show loving-kindness in some form. Whether or not it is returned to us, we need to do it. Give it to the full extent of your ability. No matter what negativity you receive back, think how lucky you are for knowing the powerful energy within you to *give.*

See chapter 5, "Strengthening Your Psychic Energy Field" for more exercises.

PART

DEVELOPMENT OF YOUR PSYCHIC ABILITIES

Intuition and Your Personal Patterns

How do I know the ways of all things at the beginning?
By what is within me.

LAO TZU

I know when I have a problem and have done all I can—
thinking, figuring, planning—I keep listening in a sort of
inside silence 'til something clicks and I feel the right answer.

CONRAD HILTON

INTUITION

Intuition is often defined as knowing something without realizing why or how you know it.

A "hunch" is a common synonym for intuition, as is being hit by lightning, having a bulb light up inside your head, having everything fall into place, feeling something in your bones, or a gut reaction. Each of these figures of speech expresses an understanding of the nature of intuition.

Sometimes intuition is thought to be a synonym (and a more acceptable term) for rudimentary ESP. "Women's intuition" may be a *cliché* that expresses that viewpoint. I feel that most women, especially mothers, are more prone to being psychic. As a child did you ever wonder how your mother knew some of the things you did?

I also feel that women who are in the menopause stage of their life are very psychic. This is my own intuition, but I feel it to be very true.

LISTENING TO THE
STILL, SMALL VOICE

How can we begin to recognize intuition? Let's start with something simple we can play with—a *yes* or *no* situation. Is this person telling me the truth? Would this be a good business investment? Is this really the career for me? Shall I take this job?

Begin with some choice or a decision that you have to make. Now use whatever resources you have that are relevant and make your choice or decision. Study the situation, examine your feelings, make a list of pros and cons. This period of preparation is important. Intuitive information can build upon the foundation of information that you collect and evaluate at the conscious level. The period of preparation also places you into a position of attunement with the area or topic of your concern. After you have studied the situation, make your decision.

When I have a decision to make on something such as the welfare of my child and what is best for her, I think seriously about that decision. And when I make the decision (if it is the right one), I feel good about it. A weight is lifted off my shoulders and no longer do I feel harried about it. If I make the wrong decision, I will know it because an intuitive hunch of right or wrong will bother me. If I am not troubled by my decision, then I know I made the right choice.

If your decision is upsetting you, then you should meditate. In the meditation, align your psychic energy vibrations to the highest ideal, which is the most universal or encompassing pattern of truth, and with the understanding that your decision is to be in harmony with that ideal. Then, bring your decision into mind and ask yourself, "Is this the right choice?" Listen to your inner reaction. The inner prompting that you receive is either a *yes* or a *no,* and this is an act of intuition. It may come to you as a feeling, a thought, or you may even hear a voice.

How your inner self will speak to you is something that you have to discover for yourself, but the response will come. I suggest this practice specifically for learning to recognize the workings of intuition. It is also a workable form of seeking guidance. I suggest developing intuition by using it in an applied manner. If you take real situations in which you care about the outcome and apply yourself to figuring out a solution consciously, and if you also seek a period of silence where you can receive, you will experience an intuitive response to your choice or decision.

INNER KNOWING

Intuition is an inner response, and the intuitive person is one who is familiar with the inner self. Intuition is an expression of the whole person; it is not just a simple technique or an isolated skill. If you are creative and have developed your psychic abilities, then your intuition will be at a much higher level than ever before. For a simple test to prove this, I will give you a situation called the Rod Test in which you are to imagine yourself. Whether you do this in your mind or actually set it up physically (with someone helping you), it is still a test of your mind and how it works. It is like the test policemen give suspected drunk drivers. They ask them to walk an imaginary line. It is not just a question of whether they can walk a straight line but also of whether their *mind* can create the straight line first. If not, their mind is not working normally. When you can do the following exercise you will know that your senses are in balance. Until then, you need to concentrate until you have a clearer picture of a stable vertical position of the rod. Practice this exercise until you have that straight line.

EXERCISE 22

Rod Test

1. You are seated in a very dark room. On the other side of the room hangs an illuminated rod—a smooth, straight stick. The rod is hanging fairly straight, in an up and down position.

2. This test doesn't measure eyesight, but whether you can determine from your inner sense when the rod is in a vertical position. To do that you have to align yourself inwardly with gravity and with the rod and make a comparison between the rod's position and your sense of the vertical. People vary in their ability to make a correct determination of the vertical.

3. The real test comes when a frame is placed around the rod. The frame is purposely just a bit off the vertical, and then you have to determine the verticality of the rod. It is easy to be misled by the frame.

4. Passing the test requires substituting what your outer-directed senses are telling you in favor of cues you are getting from your body. You need your outer-directed senses to examine the verticality of the rod, but you have to ignore what your senses are telling you about the frame. The measure of verticality has to come from within.

5. People who can determine true verticality from this test are called "field independent" because they can operate independently of the external field created by the frame. Keep practicing.

This testing procedure has been used by many psychics to predict such personality traits as creativity, openness to inner experience, dream recall, and other aspects of intuition. It is a good way to show to others what it means to be in touch with one's "inner" self.

You can actually advance your psychic abilities by practicing a thorough test with numbers. I was always good at numbers. Whenever I went to an amusement park there would be that big wheel with a lot of numbers on it. To test my skill, I would pick a number, place a quarter on it, and if it came up I would win a prize. At one time I was actually asked to leave because I won so many prizes.

Test your ability to perceive patterns, specifically number patterns. For example, if I were to say the numbers 2, 1, 2 . . . What would you say the next number would be? Easy, it's the number 1.

What about a series of numbers? Such as 1, 4, 5, 2 . . . What comes next? Not so easy, huh? What if I show you more of it: 1, 4, 5, 2, 5 . . . 6, 3, 6, and 7. What comes next? The answer is 4 (the series is made up of triplets: 4, 7, 8 comes up next). You have to actually see the number that comes next in your mind's eye before making a guess.

EXERCISE 23

Numbers Test

1. Get a mathematics book with number series in it.

2. Write down the beginning of a series—maybe ten repeats of the pattern.

3. Try to guess the next numbers.

4. Choose a different number series; write down and study nine repeats of the pattern.

5. Try to figure out the next numbers in the series.

6. Repeat with different number series until you can figure out a pattern after looking at only one set of the series. Work with someone else if necessary so that you don't get clues to the pattern ahead of time.

Practice makes perfect. You can do this with lottery numbers. If you see a pattern of numbers that comes up more frequently than any others during the course of a month, then use those numbers. Use the above exercise to practice with until you have it down pat.

When you perceive yourself to be a bit psychic, your overall traits will be creativity, confidence, self-sufficiency, independence, and spontaneity. These traits come from an identity based on personal and inner factors rather than outward perceptions. You will be resistant to outside control, willing to risk criticism, and capable of handling doubt and uncertainty. You are a bit unconventional; however, you are comfortable with it. You will score high on field independence, a trait measured by tests such as the rod experiment above.

Creativity tests can predict performance in ESP situations. For example, some of my students' abilities include prediction of a sequence of patterns that a computer would generate though a random process. Creativity tasks, such as thinking of different uses for a brick, train your psychic abilities. Word games, such as how many words can you make from one word, are useful.

EXERCISE 24
Word Test

1. Get a big piece of paper.

2. Write down the word *inspiration* at the top.

3. Write down all the words that can be made using letters from that word. (Clue: After the editor of this book spent two minutes on this, she had fifty-eight words.)

We can create our own creativity. So practice.

LEARNING TO TRUST AND USE YOUR INTUITION

You have to learn to trust your intuition and this means learning to act on it. You shouldn't have to wait until you face an important decision. Your intuition is working all of the time. Try acting on it.

Who's Calling? Sometimes You Know

To get started, try to get in the habit of announcing who the caller is every time the phone rings. When you hear the phone ring, simply speak up and declare, "That is . . . calling," blurting out whatever name comes to you. Intuition is knowing without knowing how you know. So assume an innocent-knowing frame of mind, and make the announcement aloud as if you really know who it is. If you feel hesitant, perhaps you can appreciate the results of research indicating that intuitive people are willing to take risks and are not afraid to expose themselves to criticism. Take a chance and you will be surprised.

Take a note of the results. When you are correct, note how your valid intuitions feel when they come to you. When you are incorrect, examine what was on your mind as you made your announcement. Don't get frustrated if you are wrong, that's how we learn. Perhaps you will discover that there was some thought or image connected with the person who was calling, something you suppressed or discounted. Those oversights will also teach you something of what the ingredients of intuition feel like.

Make Snap Decisions and Predictions

Are you slow to make even the most trivial decisions? Try acting quickly and spontaneously without much thought. Make quick choices about which movie to see or what to order from the menu as a means of developing the intuitive response. I enjoy making predictions about how movies will turn out or the identity of the culprit in detective stories, which is another enjoyable way to turn everyday situations into intuition games.

Change Your Habits

Habits can stifle intuition, whether they are habits of daily routine or those of rational thought. It can be helpful to alter your routine to develop the flexibility that can more readily admit the promptings of intuition. Do you drive home from work the same way everyday? Try to vary the route. Try going for a random drive and at each intersection make a spontaneous choice of direction.

Just Drive Around

Combine such experiments with your program of action for using your awakening psychic ability. As you go on a random drive be sensitive for any inner promptings to pull over and investigate some business establishment—just to visit, perhaps. You'll be surprised at how it may inform your life or career.

"I Knew I Should Have Gone the Other Way"

One time a higher energy form prompted me to pull over to the side of the road. I did; of course, it was an automatic reaction. Just beyond where I stopped a four-car pileup happened. I watched the entire fiasco and explained to the police officer exactly how it happened. I am always asked why did I pull over before it happened? I can't tell you in simple layman's terms, but I can tell you it was my psychic abilities working overtime.

Act on Your Dreams

You can also apply this approach to your dreams. Try assuming that your dreams are intuitive visions and act on them. Seek out or create experiences that correlate with your dream images. If you dream of a friend, call that person for a chat. Or, they may call you.

Let any other intuitions that might arise while you are doing such things prompt spontaneous actions, questions, and searchings. You may find yourself another step down the road to an opportunity for a new career. Working with your dreams in the intuitive way can be enhanced if you specifically attempt to "incubate" dreams as described in chapter 7, "Advanced Tools: Dreams As a Pathway."

EXPERIMENTING WITH A PENDULUM

You can discover the psychic ability of your subconscious mind by working with a pendulum. After the pendulum has helped you bypass your conscious mind and gain access to the ESP of your superconscious mind, then you should gradually dispense with the pendulum and pick up messages from your subconscious directly.

You may begin with an experiment that is done just out of curiosity, but then progress to something more in keeping with your plans for applying your psychic ability.

The use of the pendulum in ESP tests has been found to produce more accurate results than simple guessing. Try to see if you can obtain this effect yourself. Play the guess-a-card game.

EXERCISE 25

Guessing Cards

1. Have a friend sit down out of your sight, pick a card from a deck, and focus on the color red or black.

2. Guess whether it is red or black.

3. After each guess have your friend show you the card so you can see for yourself.

4. Run through a series of ten cards and keep track of your score.

5. Then switch to using a pendulum. Determine which pendulum response will represent black and which will represent red. Run through a series of ten cards with the pendulum and record the results.

6. At the end see which method was more accurate. If the pendulum can access your subconscious mind's psychic ability better than your mind can, then use the pendulum when practicing or testing your abilities. Getting eight or more out of ten right would definitely be considered beating the odds. Getting only two or less right would be considered *"negative ESP,"* meaning you are demonstrating ESP but using it to make yourself wrong. If that is the case, perhaps ESP frightens you.

7. When you have satisfied yourself that the pendulum can demonstrate ESP in guessing cards, then try to wean yourself from it altogether. Begin by seeing if you can guess in advance how the pendulum is going to respond. When you can do that without reducing the pendulum's ESP accuracy, then you are probably ready to dismiss the pendulum for card guessing.

Now try something that relates to your plan of application for using psychic abilities. Here is a suggestion concerning careers.

EXERCISE 26
Newspaper Job Search

1. Cut out some help wanted ads from your newspaper. Pick a few that relate to jobs you know you would really hate to work at and a few you think you might like. In addition, pick about twice as many jobs you aren't sure about.

2. Paste each job on an index card.

3. Then take the pendulum and establish its response code. Perhaps left to right would mean, "I might not do well at this job," and swinging in a clockwise circular pattern would mean, "I would definitely like this job," while swinging in a counterclockwise pattern would mean, "I would not like this job." No movement would indicate, "No opinion." This is not like one of those eight balls that you shake and it states, "Not at this time"—this is the real thing!

4. The choice of responses should be based on the type of questions you are concerned with, such as career preferences, innate abilities, hunches that the job would lead to something good, prospects of being hired, and so forth.

5. Once the pendulum response code is established, reach for each want ad in turn (you look at the pendulum

while doing this), and note your pendulum response. See if it correlates with your conscious opinion. When it doesn't, try it again. If the pendulum continues to give you a consistent response, but one that is different from your conscious opinion, you may have something to think about.

6. To test for ESP results, have your friend pick up one of these cards at random and silently read it while thinking about you in connection with such a job. Check your pendulum response to the card now, when only your friend knows its identity. If the pendulum tends to make the same response to the job card whether you are looking at the card, or whether your friend is looking at it and you don't know the card's identity, you are getting some interesting ESP effects.

7. Have your friend run through the cards a few times and find cards that your pendulum responds to in a consistent manner. This is a very interesting ESP effect, one that can have some potential meaning for you in terms of career questions. Those job cards must relate to careers to which your subconscious mind for some reason is very sensitive.

8. Compare your feelings about these jobs with your friend's impressions of your abilities, preferences, and so forth, which your pendulum may have been picking up on.

Here is an example from my own life. When I was younger I drew a circle and around the circle placed the numbers one to six. I let a pendulum swing from side to side over these numbers, and I asked "How many children will I have?" It answered five. I do have five children, four girls and one boy. I did that experiment more than thirty years ago.

The primary value of the pendulum is its ability to demonstrate the ESP ability of your subconscious mind prior to your being able to experience psychic imagery. The pendulum should be recognized, however, for the automatism that it is. It is not a tool favored by the most professional psychic workers because of the problem of opening up oneself to outside influence. However, in contrast to automatic writing and the Ouija board, the pendulum allows only a limited degree of conscious dissociation; therefore it is not particularly dangerous if you don't rely on it as a substitute for developing your own psychic abilities.

The pendulum serves to amplify the reaction of your subconscious mind and to make it more visible to the eye. Having thus seen that our subconscious is responding psychically, you should be able to develop the mental equivalent of the pendulum by focusing on your feelings and imagery, which will be discussed in more detail later in this chapter.

MENTAL TELEPATHY

Sending telepathic messages is a way of life. It will certainly increase your intuitive powers, but it will also give you an overall feeling of connectedness that is very rewarding. It can deepen relationships you already have. And it involves you in some important information sharing.

Here is the key to telepathic awareness, which I learned through an experiment from a close friend of mine—regular message sending.

EXERCISE 27
The Daily Posting

1. Arrange with a friend to set aside some time each day when the both of you, each in your own particular location, can sit quietly and try to tune in on the other person.

2. Allow your mind to resonate with the other person's experience (thoughts, recent activities, feelings, surroundings, plans, and so forth), and make notes or diagrams on what you pick up.

3. You are actually picking up on your friend's own vibrations or psychic energy level. If it is high, and yours is high, you will have no problem in communicating. This can work even if one person's energy is high and the other's is low.

4. Check in with each other regularly in between the daily experiments and compare notes.

5. I suggest trying this experiment for thirty days in a row, at about the same time of the day or night. You should see some results within that time period.

The merits of this approach to investigating telepathy have been repeatedly validated. It was made famous by

Upton Sinclair, who worked with his wife over a long period of time and wrote of their experiences in his book, *Mental Radio.*

I also suggest setting aside some time to develop the "spontaneity of intuition." An example of spontaneity of intuition is the recurrence of patterns, either in sequence or sporadically. Success will follow your persistence.

CHANNELING

Channeling is a form of intuition, an "inner process," a connection with an unseen source of information and insight. Channeling can be defined as, "the ability to act as a vehicle for thoughts, feelings, images, and information coming from sources beyond the individual self and ordinary reality as we think we know it, a source that is not identifiable and that may not identify itself." Creativity and inspiration are forms of channeling.

Contacting the higher self, connecting with cosmic consciousness, soul contact, are all terms that are interchangeable with channeling.

As with other forms of intuition, the open channeling we call intuition often occurs in response to a need. It is a source of information and insight. A need here is described as wanting or requiring something that is not a material good. For instance, how can we get things done on time when we have no help? Did you ever have a large driveway that needed to be shoveled of snow? You are the only one to do it, and you need help. So you channel a connection to an unseen source, and you swear that you were able to finish quickly because an unseen force helped you.

As a psychic reader, I sometimes have to look to my inner self to see the distinct wholeness of the person I am facing. I generally do not use tarot cards, palm reading, or anything material. I have to look into my inner self and feel the energy vibrations from the other person, and immediately I am able to tell what is going on in his life, what problems exist, if any, and just about everything about that person as a whole. Sometimes people try to fool me and tell me there is nothing bothering them, when in fact I always tell them what it is. I don't have to pry any information from them, and when I say statements to them that are true, they know it, even if they don't want to know.

I cannot direct the course of life for anyone. I cannot tell Jane or Sally if she is going to marry Bob or Joe. But I can advise her about what kind of energies I am receiving from the people in her life. If I am asked to do a reading about a person in her life, it is hard for me to give a reading as I have to feel the specific energies about me. Sometimes, though, it is possible to work with just a piece of clothing or a picture.

Psychic intuition—everyone has it. You just have to develop it more fully.

FEELINGS AND IMAGES

I am going to suggest an experiment that responds to one's inner self. Intuition and its still, small voice may come in a variety of guises, including feelings and images. These can be the manifestation of the inner voice providing intuitive information. When we are concerned about a particular topic or situation, we become attuned to it—our being begins to resonate to the vibrations of the situation. Our inner self begins to manifest the effects of that resonance by producing analogous patterns of its own in the form of feelings and images.

Take Albert Einstein. He gave free rein to his imagination. Always pondering the nature of time, he imagined being a clock that was hurtling through space, traveling faster and faster. That image led him to the relativity theory. Another famous example is Kekulé's discovery of the formula of the benzene ring. Pondering the nature of organic compounds, he found himself imagining a snake curled back on itself, biting its tail. He recognized in the image the pattern for the formula he was seeking. In such cases of scientific discoveries, the seekers were so intently involved with the problem at hand they unconsciously became "one with" the object of study. Their whole being— their thinking, their feelings and imagination—launched into an impromptu commentary.

Recently a close friend of mine asked me if she would ever get her "dream" house, so I told her to imagine it. Imagine what kind of house you want to live in, what the property looks like, the furniture, everything about it, and keep thinking about it , and it will come to you. Most of the time it will take anywhere between one and five years, or it may sometimes occur overnight, but eventually what you think about, if you always use positive energy, will direct that positive energy to make your dreams come true. The same holds true for your health. In 1994 I had breast cancer, and I directed all of my energy toward getting better even though I felt awful. I never suffered the consequences of chemotherapy or radiation, thank God. I am now five years cancer-free and still going strong. For me, this has to do with God and directing positive energy and thoughts on wellness.

Listening to that still, small voice plays a big part, like knowing something without knowing how we know it.

Have you ever had the experience of making a statement with conviction then afterwards marveled at the truth of what you said, asking yourself, "How did I know that?" This is a common occurrence for those on the path of psychic development

HOW TO GET IN TOUCH
WITH DEEPER FEELINGS

Have you ever had a powerful yearning for something, such as wanting someone to love you back, craving a special type of food, or acquiring money for a bill that is due? Yet, you say to yourself, this is impossible—there is no way this can come about? *Oh ye, of such little faith.* Think of what you need in your life that is most important. Don't pick something that is here today, gone tomorrow. Think of what you truly desire. A passion, a deep-seated feeling—

see it in your mind's eye. When you can see it—that is what faith is, seeing it in your mind and knowing it in your heart—it will come to pass.

There was a time when I wanted to live in a nice mobile home. There were many people who had their name on a list with the landlord, so it seemed I had no chance. But still I imagined it in my mind, and it did come to pass. Of course this faith is guided by your deepest feelings, and it is intended to be directed towards real needs, such as staying healthy. Don't try to use your energy for a sports car or a zillion dollars. Think realistically, along the lines of enjoying a long life or wishing for the happiness of your loved ones. Think positively about what you would like to have in your life, and it will eventually come to pass. If you are ill, you may want to think about the antibodies in your body killing and fighting germs or bad cells. Imagine becoming the healthiest person there ever could be.

Here is a short exercise to help you find lost items. It can also be used to find lost people. When I needed to find my husband's wallet, I would sit down and mentally ask my inner self where he had hidden it.

EXERCISE 28
Finding Lost Items

1. Sit in a quiet part of your home.

2. Close your eyes gently.

3. Have a friend hide various items for you.

4. Say to your inner self whatever your question is. Always go with your first answer. Do not actually go and look for the item. Ask your friend if you are correct.

5. Even if you fail, take a deep breath, relax, and start over. Patience and persistence will pay off.

How to Relax and Allow Images to Form

Daydreaming is okay! More than okay, it is necessary for mental and physical health and for the growth of the individual, especially spiritually.

EXERCISE 29
Conjuring Up Useful Images

Have you ever had a daydream while you were in your car and wondered why you never got in an accident while driving from one place to another? Oftentimes, while I am driving to the college where I teach part-time, I will be daydreaming of what I will say to the students or wondering if there are any lessons that I still need to give them, all the while driving. It's an automatic reaction to stop suddenly, to turn a corner, or to jolt suddenly when someone honks a horn. This happens to all of us even if it is not recognized at the time.

A constructive daydream can happen at any time. When you are relaxed, your thoughts can drift. In this more concentrated and relaxed state of mind, when you are not worrying and there is little external noise, your daydreams may bring you a better perspective. You may get in touch with things that are coming into fruition.

How to Interpret Feelings and Images

Our inner feelings or gut feelings are those that we need to pay more attention to. If you feel that something is not right, then it probably isn't. If you are worried about someone you haven't heard from in a while, then you should do something. No matter what is bothering you, you can avoid confusion by getting into a relaxed state and asking yourself about your inner concerns.

These inner concerns can become visions. When you see a vision, you can act upon it. Don't ask whether it is a good vision or a bad vision. Act upon your first thought. If you don't, you will usually be sorry later. We are almost always right in acting upon our visions.

Here is another feeling you may have. The vibrant feeling of life, a happy feeling that may lead you through the worst days. Act on these feelings. More than ever before, I feel that everyday life needs to be celebrated. Be joyous. Be alive. Regardless of the troubles and woes of this planet, and of those living on it, life is for celebrating each and every day. Make the most of it and spread the joy to others.

If you don't have much feeling or feel cold and numb, then I suggest you get some help, even if from a book. I truly believe that we when we look at other people's problems, we see how blessed we are. And as we start to get this great feeling of gratitude, maybe we can help those not as blessed.

Feelings: Grab on, Then Let Go

Feelings are not the real goal, merely a means. We don't want our lives to get hung up on feelings, which we could investigate forever. They are another tool, another source of information about ourselves and the world, but sometimes feelings interfere with deeper information from our soul and other sources. It is up to us to decide which is true and which is not, and we can only do this by knowing ourselves, especially our inner selves.

Always look at feelings and images in the largest context possible. We do not run out and act on every feeling that emerges. We look at its overall meaning in our lives. Some feelings just need to be let go of, others can be informative, still others give us direction.

THE EXAMPLE OF WRITING

Let's consider three forms of writing. The first is conscious, intentional writing, as I am doing now. This is what we all do on our first attempt, as with the first attempt at observing our breath. We feel we are in control, that we have to think up what we should write about, and we are conscious of our choice of words or our lack of words to express what is in our minds. We sit back and try to think up something to write and then write it down. That is intentional writing.

Another form is automatic writing. Just as we can breathe automatically without paying attention to the process, it is possible for some people to write without paying any attention to their writing. By distracting, blocking, or blanketing the mind, they have learned to let the "unconscious speak directly" through their writing. Automatic writing is a form of channeling that should be avoided. For instance, in automatic breathing, when we become upset our breath responds accordingly. Sometimes we breathe fast, and sometimes we actually stop breathing or hold back the breath—the breath expresses the problem or the upset. In much the same way, automatic writing can express discord, fear, and groping in a person's life. Or it can express power strivings, struggles to achieve—to "get on top" or "get one's way." It can be seductive. It doesn't necessarily express the best, nor is it the most creative.

The third form, inspirational writing, is like observing your breathing without interfering with it. With inspirational writing, you are aware of the purpose of the writing, you are aware of what you write as you write it, but you experience the writing as almost happening by itself. It is a higher form of automatic writing.

To perform inspirational writing, you reverse the usual procedure. Normally in conscious, intentional writing, you first think of what you want to say, and then you record your thoughts. In inspirational writing you do the reverse: You begin writing with your purpose in mind and you observe what you write, just as I am doing right now. You are not recording your thoughts on paper, but rather you are noting awareness in what you write.

To make sure that you don't get caught up in automatic writing instead of inspirational writing, you must prepare. To prepare for inspirational writing, it helps to focus on your breathing for a moment before you begin each writing exercise, reminding yourself that you can be aware of your breathing without stopping the flow. Before you begin it is important to meditate. In meditation try to quiet the mind and tune into your highest thoughts. Highest means the most universal perspective. Think of the little white tornado circling above your head to clear away any unwanted thoughts and negative feelings. With meditation comes the sense of peace and of being at one with life. Often questions are posed and a very different sort of answer is given. Meditation itself is a form of channeling. We channel the creative forces that flow throughout our bodies.

EXERCISE 30
Inspirational Writing

1. I suggest an atmosphere of dim lighting, perhaps some quiet music, such as nature's sounds, and incense if appropriate. Incense and light, mystical music elevate your state of consciousness to a higher vibrational energy.

2. Then set your pen to paper. Following the ideas I have set forth about intuition operating on a need-to-know basis, it is better to choose a topic that concerns you deeply.

If you will listen or accept what is there, the ideas will emerge for you to set down on paper. Simply begin to write, noting what is being written; don't wait for the experience of being dictated to, just write anything that comes to your mind.

I would like to suggest "getting in touch" with your intuitional inner self and how it may appear to you. You should also be very sensitive to your inner promptings. If your "inner voice" or "inner self" tells you to write, then do it. It is almost like listening to your mother or someone else directing your path. If you fail to respond or take it seriously, you will know you should have listened to that inner voice when the time comes and something happens.

CHAPTER

Strengthening Your Psychic Energy Field

Remember in the beginning of this book I mentioned how someone could "borrow" or steal your energy away from you?

At some point in your evolution, you come to the realization that you are made of more than just the physical body. You begin to understand that there is more to the world than meets the eye. Most people focus their concentration on things that are visible and tangible, but science is proving that many things that are not visible to the human eye affect us.

If you are unaware of how extraneous forces can affect you, you can end up with weaknesses in your own energy system. These weaknesses may manifest as actual physical illnesses or as mental/emotional imbalances. Your individual energy system is imposed and impinged upon every day. Unless you learn to recognize this phenomenon and work to protect yourself from unwanted intrusions, you may find your life becoming more complicated.

We have all had experiences in which our energies were affected by outside forces. Extraneous sounds, heat, and electrical impositions occur frequently. Other individuals impinge upon your energies as well. Has anyone ever made you feel that you were inferior or a failure? Have you ever been influenced to purchase something or participate in an activity when you really did not want to? Have you ever felt drained after talking with another person? All of these are intrusions upon your energy field. The key to protecting your energies lies with the psychic energy field within yourself. With a strong and vibrant field, negative, draining, and unbalanced energies are deflected. Maintaining a strong energy field is not difficult.

GENERAL FACTORS AND TOOLS

Environment, lifestyle, emotions, stress, values, time management, and physical habits all profoundly affect your energy field.

Most beneficial to the energy field are positive health practices. Proper diet, exercise, and fresh air are strengthening to the entire psychic energy field. On the other hand, the lack of these things can and will tear a hole in your energy field and make you feel weak and depressed.

Your psychic energy field is extremely affected by emotional and mental states, more than you can imagine. A weakened energy field results in energy drains. You become tired more easily. If the drain is prolonged, holes and tears occur within the fabric of your energy field.

Physical health problems will begin to manifest, along with other imbalances. There are many simple ways of vitalizing and strengthening the human psychic energy field. Sunlight is strengthening to the energy field. So is physical exercise. Fresh air is vitalizing and has a more balanced effect on your energy field. Keeping the bowels clean assists in keeping your psychic energy field strong and resilient. Meditation is also strengthening and protective. You do not have to become excessive in these practices. Moderation in all things is beneficial to keeping the psychic energy field vibrant.

Music can also be used to balance and strengthen the energy field. Gregorian chants are very cleansing to negative energies in the psyche or within the environment. Recently I purchased a cassette called *Sounds of Ponds and Streams*. I sat on the floor, crossed my knees to my chest, and listened to the sounds of running water in a brook, birds chirping, and the sound of the wind. I actually felt the wind on my face, and the babbling brook and I became one.

We have all had experiences when we walk into a room in which there has been a fight or an argument. The air is thick; you can feel the tension. Playing a Gregorian chant for about ten minutes within the room can cleanse it of any negative energy. Chants will also do the same for your energy field. Some people have difficulty with the music of these chants for various personal reasons and tastes. If that is your case, use any piece of classical music that you find uplifting and soothing.

Fragrances can also be used to protect and strengthen the energy field. Smudging in the Native American tradition is common. Smudging is the practice of using the smoke and fragrance of various herbs to cleanse the energy field or the environment.

Another tool for protecting and strengthening the psychic energy field is a quartz crystal or stone. The electrical energy inherent within a crystal will amplify and strengthen the psychic energy field as well. A good experiment to prove this is to have someone measure your psychic energy field (and this can really be done by "washing your hands" without water) and then with one crystal in your hand after the dry wash you will be able to feel the energy transfer to the crystal. Place the crystal down on a table, then place your hands near the crystal and watch it move ever so slightly.

If you have a quartz crystal with points on both ends, it can be extremely effective for strengthening your psychic energy level. Carrying one in your pocket can actually stabilize your energy level, too. This is effective especially if you know you will be going into a tense meeting or a draining situation.

At the end of the day when you find yourself drained or just wishing to regain your energy level, sit or stand with a double-sided quartz crystal in both hands. Then relax and visualize the energy of the crystal recharging your body and increasing your energy level. Do this for at least five to ten minutes. This practice helps leave the office stuff behind because it cleanses the psychic energy field of energy debris that you carried out of the office with you.

OFF THE TOP

Quickly and intuitively answer the questions:

What one thing do you know works for you and always increases your energy? What else? _____

_____

What is the most draining thing you do? _____

_____

Anything else? _____

_____

EXERCISE 31

Energy and Everyday Activities Chart

Nature/Spirit	Work	Family	Relationships	Religion/Grace
Strengthening				
Direction				
Receiving				
Gathering				
Combining				
Draining				
Results				

1. Make a chart like this one of what strengthens and what weakens you. Mark where your energy has gone for the past week. Where was it directed? Did you receive back any strong vibrations? At what point were you gathering it together as a whole? Were you able to gather all the pieces together at any one point? Where were you drained?

2. Do this exercise every two to four weeks. Check your results and see where you need to better direct your energies to benefit yourself or others.

TECHNIQUES FOR BOOSTING OR MAINTAINING ENERGY

The following exercises are beneficial for protecting and strengthening your energy field. They help balance and energize you. They also help prevent intrusion from unwanted forces and energies. The stronger and more vibrant you keep your psychic energy field, the less you will have your energies intruded upon.

EXERCISE 32
Preventing Yourself from Being Drained

We have all experienced being drained by another person. You may talk to him on the phone or in person, and when you finish you are exhausted. You feel completely drained; your energy is gone; your stomach may ache, etc. What you are experiencing is an energy drain. Some individuals draw or suck off the energy of others. Most of the time the individuals involved do not realize it. In many cases they are using your energies to supplement their own because they are unable to build up their own. All they may realize is that when they finish talking or being with you they feel better. This does not give them the right to take your energy, however, and you should not allow it.

This does not mean that you should accuse this person of being a vampire or say that he is sucking off your energy. If you do, he will think you have gone off the deep end. In that case, your problem will be solved because he will probably not care to see you after that. In any case, your energy is your responsibility, and you cannot expect others to necessarily understand the subtler aspects.

You correct the situation by deciding whether to share your energy or not. One of the simplest methods is to close your circuit of energy. There are currents of energy flowing through your body and around it within your psychic energy field. You can close them down so that your energies only circulate around your own psychic field and throughout your body. You prevent your energies from being drawn off, and you prevent your energy from drawing in another's energy.

Assuming the safe posture is all it takes. Cross your feet at the ankles and bring your thumbs and fingers together so they are touching. (If you wish, you can use just the thumbs and index fingers.) This closes your circuit. Your energy will not go out from you.

The next time you encounter your friend who drains you assume this posture. Simply rest your hands casually on your lap, touch your fingers, and cross your ankles. It is casual and simple and no one will suspect you of anything. You can also do this when you're on the phone with such people.

If you do this you may get some feedback through other friends as to the effects. You may hear comments such as "You're not as nice," or "You are not as open as you used to be," or " I wonder if so and so is mad at me," etc.

You will still be talking with them as nicely and as often as ever. What you are not doing is allowing them to take your energy! You simply are not allowing them to drain you. Because they are not getting "high" from you, they are assuming something is wrong. No one has the right to take your energy without your permission.

EXERCISE 33
Energy Breathing Technique

Fresh air and proper breathing are essential to a strong and vital psyche. Breathing for maximum energy to the energy field should be done through the nostrils. Many people have a bad habit of mouth breathing, not realizing that nostril breathing is more natural and healthy.

Mouth breathing makes an individual more susceptible to diseases. It impairs the vitality of the psychic energy field. It can even weaken the constitution. Between the mouth and the lungs there is nothing to strain the air. Dust, dirt, and other impure substances have a clear track to the lungs. Mouth breathing also admits cold air to the lungs, which can lead to inflammation of the respiratory organs.

Nostril breathing, on the other hand, is more vitalizing and healthy to your entire energy system. The nose provides specialized surfaces for absorption of *prana* from the air. *Prana* can be likened to the vitalizing aspect that exists within the air. Many Eastern breathing techniques require a conscious focus upon the tip of the nose and the entire nasal area during inhalation. This enhances the *prana* absorption, raises the vitality of the entire energy level, and stimulates the entire energy system of the human being.

The nostrils and the nasal passages are designed with hair to filter and sieve the air. They also warm the air through the mucous membranes, making it fit for the delicate organs of the lungs. Breath is then more energizing and strengthening to your psychic level.

In yoga the moon breath is termed the *Ida* and the sun breath is termed the *Pingala*. The balance of the two is *Sushumma*. Your energy has polarity: positive and negative, male and female, sun and moon. This breathing technique quickly energizes the psychic energy field and balances the polarity of the body. It also enhances your ability to remember and assimilate information.

The moon breath balances the hemispheres of the brain. It can be used before studying to shorten learning time. It can be used as a quick pick-me-up during the day. (Remember that conscious attention to the tip of the nose, especially during the inbreath, will magnify the effects of these techniques.) The rhythm is aided by holding the nose with the thumb and forefinger.

1. Exhale while holding your nostrils shut with your right thumb and fingers. Place your tongue against the roof of your mouth behind your front teeth.

2. Use your thumb and close your right nostril; then inhale through your left nostril for a slow count of four.

3. Keeping your right nostril closed, clamp your fingers down over your left nostril, pinching your nose closed between your thumb and forefingers. Hold for a count of sixteen. (If you have never performed any concentrated rhythmic breathing, the count of sixteen may be too long for you. If this is the case, reduce it or count faster.) With practice, you will develop the ability to hold your breath for more extended periods. Try inhaling for a count of three, holding for a count of six and then exhaling for a count of three. Work to find the rhythm that is most effective for you and then build upon it.

4. Release your thumb, opening your right nostril, and keep your left nostril closed with your fingers. Exhale slowly out through your right nostril for a count of eight.

5. Release your nose; raise your left hand up and with your thumb, close off your left nostril. Inhale for a count of four through your right nostril and then clamp your fingers closed on it. Hold for a count of sixteen.

6. Release your thumb and your left nostril. Keep your right nostril clamped with your fingers. Exhale for a slow count of eight through your left nostril.

7. Repeat four to five times, alternating each side. Breathe in one nostril, hold, and exhale out the other. This will saturate your entire body and psychic energy field with quick energy.

EXERCISE 34
The Cleansing Vortex

Figure 5 depicts a visualization exercise for cleansing and purifying your entire energy field. It is an excellent exercise to perform at the end of the day, especially at those times when you have interacted with a great many people. It helps sweep out the energy debris, preventing it from accumulating and creating imbalance within the energy field. It only takes about five minutes to be effective.

1. Sit and perform a progressive relaxation. Performing the breathing technique just described is beneficial as a preparation for this exercise. You may want to use a simple prayer or mantra as well. Remember that the exercise as presented here is just a guideline and you should learn to adapt it to your own energies.

2. Visualize in your mind's eye a small whirlwind of crystalline white fire beginning to form about twenty feet above you. It looks like a small, spiritual tornado. As it forms its funnel shape, visualize it so that it is large

Figure 5. The Cleansing Vortex

enough to encompass your entire energy field. The small end of the funnel should be visualized passing down the middle pillar of your body.

3. This whirlwind of spiritual fire should be seen as rotating and spinning clockwise. As it touches upon your energy, see it sucking up and burning off all of the energy debris you have accumulated. This may take a while if you have a lot of accumulation of energy debris.

4. See, feel, and imagine it moving down, over, and through your entire energy field and body. Know that it is sweeping your energy field clean of all the extraneous energies you have accumulated throughout the day.

5. As it moves through your body, allow this energy vortex to exit out through your feet and down into the heart of the earth itself. See the vortex as it carries the energy debris into the lower realms where it is used to fertilize and benefit the lower kingdoms of life upon and within the planet.

If you have ever seen sparks fly from a grinding wheel, you can just imagine what the energy debris looks like.

EXERCISE 35
The Middle Pillar Exercise

I have not found another single exercise that can do so much and adapt itself so well to the individual.

I teach this exercise in my workshops and stress it as absolutely fundamental. It should be employed by anyone wishing to open up her higher faculties. It is so powerful and so effective that it should become the staple of those just beginning as well as those who have involved themselves in the metaphysical field for years. It is grounding, protective, and strengthening.

This exercise is drawn from an ancient system of development known as the mystical Qabala. It employs sound, visualization, and breathing to pump your psychic energy field with tremendous amounts of energy. It helps seal leaks and holes within your energy field. The Qabala stabilizes and balances your psyche. It increases your energy levels so that you have greater amounts with which to carry out your daily tasks. It prevents your energies from being overtapped.

The exercise involves using ancient Hebrew names for God like mantras in conjunction with specific images and breathing. This combination creates what is called a synergistic effect, boosting the outcome not just three times but actually eight times. The three aspects of it (the names, the imagining, and the breathing) increase the energy exponentially (in this case, two to the third power).

1. Assume a sitting or standing position. Take a few moments to relax.

2. Visualize a crystalline white sphere of light gently coming toward you from the heavens until it is just over your head. It is vibrant and alive with energy. As you vi-

brate the following name, see and feel this light growing with intensity and filling the entire head region of your body.

3. Softly sound the name EHEIEHUH (Eh-huh-yeh). Emphasize each syllable, feeling the crown of your head come alive with energy. Repeat this name five to ten times. This name translates as, *"I am that I am."*

4. Pause and visualize a shaft of light descending from this sphere, pouring down toward the throat area of your body where a second sphere of light forms. As you vibrate aloud the God-name, YHVH ELOHIM (Yah-hoh-vah-eh-loh-heem), this sphere of light grows more vibrant and brilliant. Vibrate this name five to ten times. This name means, *"The Lord God of Creation."*

5. Pause and visualize a shaft of light descending from this sphere down to the heart area of the body. Here a third sphere of brilliant light forms. Slowly, syllable by syllable, vibrate the God-name YHVH ELOAH VADAATH (Yah-hoh-vah-eh-loh-ah-vuh-dahth). Repeat this five to ten times feeling the sphere of light grow stronger and filling that part of your body. This names means, *"God made manifest in the mind."*

6. Pause and visualize a shaft of light descending from this sphere of light down to the area of your groin. See and feel a fourth sphere of light form itself with brilliance. Vibrate the God-name SHADDAI EL CHAI (Shad-dye-el-keye) slowly five to ten times. Feel the energy coming

alive within this area of the body. This name means, *"The Almighty Living God."*

7. Pause and visualize the shaft of light descending from this fourth sphere of light down to the area of your feet. Here a fifth sphere forms, while the shaft descends down into the heart of the earth itself. As you vibrate the sound of the God-name ADONAI HAARETZ HEH (Ah-doh-nye-hah-ah-retz-hey), the sphere grows with crystalline brilliance. Repeat this five to ten times. This name means, *"Lord Of The Earth."*

8. You now have formed the Middle Pillar through your entire body and your psychic energy field. Bring your attention back to the crown of your head and begin rhythmic breathing. As you exhale slowly to a count of four, see and feel energy pour down the left side of your body, radiating outward, strengthening your psychic energy field on that side of your body. You may also feel a little bit heavier on that side as well. Inhale for a count of four and draw energy up the right side of your body from your feet to the crown of your head. See and feel this energy radiating outward, strengthening your energy field on that side of your body. Hold your breath for a count of four, and then repeat the exhalation. Do this four or five times.

9. Now as you exhale see and feel the energy stream down the front of your body for a count of four. Inhale and allow it to stream up the back. Hold it for a count of four

and repeat four to five times. You have now strengthened your entire psychic energy field. Feel this energy
surrounding you. Know that it has sealed up any leaks.
Know that it has replaced any lost energy.

10. Now feel the energy gathering at your feet. As you inhale draw rainbow-colored light up through your feet,
up through that middle pillar to the crown of your
head. As you exhale spray that rainbow light out the
top of your head to fill your entire psychic energy field
with its color and energy. It's normal to see a rainbow
spray of energy specks jump out from the energy field.
Pause and allow yourself to bask in this brilliant and renewed energy field.

The Middle Pillar Exercise is also cleansing to the entire
energy field. This exercise strengthens the field and facilitates the development of higher energies, including your
own psychic abilities. Because it raises the energy of the individual to such a high level, it also helps in the development of vision of the energy field. It increases overall
perception and sensitivity—physical and otherwise.

Traditionally, with the Middle Pillar Exercise five
spheres of light are used. A dynamic variation is to incorporate a sixth. This sixth sphere of light is activated
in the area of the third eye or brow center. This main
center is linked to physical vision (clairvoyance). This
particular variation is even more dynamic, stimulating
auric vision.

EXERCISE 36

Variation to the Middle Pillar

1. Begin as before in a sitting position. Close your eyes and relax. Listen to relaxing music.

2. Visualize the crystalline ball of light descending from the heavens to come and rest at the crown of your head. As you vibrate the name EHEIEHUH (Eh-huh-yeh), feel the crown of your head come alive with energy. You may even feel a slight tingling or a needles-and-pins sensation. Repeat this five to ten times.

3. Visualize a shaft of light descending from this sphere to form a second sphere in the area of your brow. Intone the God-name JEHOVAH (Yah-hoh-vah) softly. Visualize the sound carrying to the ends of the universe and back. Feel your inner eyes coming alive with energy. You may feel light-headed, but it will last only a few seconds. Repeat this five to ten times.

4. From this sphere, the shaft of light descends further to form a third sphere of light in the area of your throat. Vibrate the God-name JEHOVAH ELOHIM (Yah-hoh-vah-eh-loh-heem). See and feel this sphere of light come to life with brilliant vibrancy. Your throat will feel scratchy as if you have a sore throat; swallow hard and then repeat this exercise five to ten times.

5. From this sphere the shaft descends and forms a fourth sphere of light in the area of your heart. It comes alive with each intonation of the God-name JEHOVAH ELOAH

VADAATH (Yah-hoh-vah-eh-loh-ah-vuh-daath). You may have some heart palpitations, but nothing to worry about. This lasts for a few seconds. Repeat this five to ten times. You will know it is working if you feel heart palpitations and the palms of your hands get sweaty.

6. Pause and visualize the shaft of light descending from the heart sphere to the area of your groin. There, a fifth sphere of light forms. See it form and radiate brilliance with each intonation of the God-name SHADDAI EL CHAI (Shad-dye-el-keye). You will get a warm feeling in the groin area from this exercise that will last only a few seconds.

7. Again pause, and then visualize the shaft of light descending from this fifth sphere down to your feet. Here a sixth sphere of light forms, and the shaft continues down into the heart of the planet. As you intone the God-name ADONAI HAARETZ HEH (Ah-doh-nyc-hah-ah-retz-hey), see this sixth sphere of light coming to life for you. You will feel a tingling sensation in your feet.

8. You have now formed a Middle Pillar of Light that extends from the heavens to the Earth through your psychic energy field. You have activated the inner centers of light that will strengthen and protect your energy field and help awaken the inner psyche. Now perform the rhythmic breathing and visualization as outlined in the description of the traditional Middle Pillar (steps 8, 9, and 10 in Exercise 35).

Chanting for Your Psyche

Mantras and chants have been employed by the esoteric tradition in the East and in the West. They are powerful tools for energizing and strengthening.

Mantra is a Sanskrit word, and it is comparable in meaning to the English words *charm* or *spell*. With mantras and chants the power of sound is employed for particular purposes. Mantras and chants have been used to change the energy field of individuals for healing and for higher levels of consciousness.

Chants or mantras, used effectively, change the body, mind, emotions, or spirit of the individual to some degree. The sounds stimulate the energies around and within you. The vibration of a chant or mantra will have a purifying and refining affect upon your psychic field. It's similar to the ozone layer of the Earth; however, the psychic energy field is that electrifying magnetism within your body and not the Earth's. The chants or mantras work usually for one of four reasons. They work simply because of an individual's faith that they will. They work because you associate definite ideas with the sounds, which then intensify the changing of your energies. They work also because of what they mean. The meaning rhythmically beats upon your mental body, resulting in an impression being formulated within your own energy patterns. Many mantras and chants work because of their sounds alone, regardless of meaning. The sounds impinge upon your psychic energy field, creating changes within it.

Chanting is the process that releases energy through the recital of mystical words and sounds that are mysterious and powerful. The rhythm of the chanting is critical.

Chanted mantras have dynamic, dramatic effects. The number of times needed to chant a mantra before it takes effect is often debated. As in most things you must decide what works best for you. Ten to fifteen minutes of a particular chant is usually enough to experience its effects.

Working with chants and mantras is simple. Choose a mantra and familiarize yourself with its significance if you can. Choose a time during which you will not be disturbed and allow yourself to relax. Begin chanting, syllable by syllable. Allow the mantra to find its own rhythm, one that is comfortable for you.

When you stop you should still hear the mantra echoing within your mind. It will be like an old song to you after awhile. Meditate upon the energies associated with that mantra. Focus on how much more light and energy has been awakened within and around you. See your psychic energy touching others with greater vibrancy.

Sample Mantras

1. *OM.* This mantra is considered the most powerful mantra of all. It corresponds to the Egyptian *Amen* and actually represents the name of the divine Logos. OM is the Sanskrit word for the spark of life itself, that part of the divine imprisoned within physical life.

It is believed by many that there are several hundred ways of pronouncing and intoning the word OM—each with its own unique effect upon your psychic energy level. When you emphasize and prolong the "O," you affect others and your own psychic field. When the "M" (humming sound) is prolonged, the entire effect is produced more internally.

When you sound the OM, you need to see yourself rising from the domination of physical life altogether. You need to visualize your limiting and hindering thought-forms as being shattered. You need to see the energy debris you have accumulated within your psyche cleansed. OM is the sound of contact with the divine, and thus it is an instrument for freeing your energies. It has the power to cleanse, create, and release new energy so that you can move on to higher expressions of energy.

OM is also a call to attention. It settles and stabilizes your psyche. It arranges the particles of your subtle bodies into alignment. All of your energy responds to this sound. When these energies are aligned you can more easily restore health and gain a greater benefit from meditation.

A variation of OM is AUM (Au-oh-mm). This form enhances your visualization of your psyche, and it enables your thoughts to become more crystallized. It is an affirmation that your energies are at their highest and continually growing higher, as if you are saying to yourself on a primal level, "So let it be!"

AUM also helps repair weaknesses and holes within your psychic energy field. A good visualization to perform with the chanting of OM is to envision the Sanskrit letters for OM overlaying your physical body.

By repeating these chants you will find that your energy reserves will be greater and encounters with other energies will be less likely to impinge upon your own psychic energy field.

2. *OM MANI PADME HUM* (Ohm-mah-nee-pod-may-hum). This mantra literally translates as "the jewel in the lotus." It is one of the more popular mantras, and it has a variety of meanings. It is believed to be a link to the energies of the Chinese Goddess Kwan Yin. Kwan Yin is to the East what Mother Mary is to the West. She is the protector and the healer of children. Legend has it that as she achieved enlightenment and began to ascend from the earthly plane, she heard a human cry and chose to stay behind to assist humanity. Legend also states that she can negate any violence directed at anyone, and she is able to walk through legions of demons and never be harmed or swayed. This mantra acts as a protective force within the psyche. It strengthens all energy reserves and helps to prevent you from being drained or taken advantage of. This particular mantra is good to use before entering into emotional situations or places where you know tensions can run high. It makes the psyche strong enough to prevent others from

intruding upon you, physically or otherwise. The six sylla-
bles of the mantra activate energies for transforming the
debris within your psychic energy field into a purified
force. It balances emotions and assists in healing the body.

OM—This is the totality of existence and of sound. It is
the call signal. Through resonating this part of the mantra,
you can set up a link between your psychic energy field
and that of the one called Kwan Yin.

MANI—This literally means *"jewel."* It refers to a kind of
non-substance that is impervious to harm or change. It is a
symbol of the highest value within the mind. It symbolizes
enlightenment with compassion and love. Just as a jewel
can remove poverty, this aspect of the mantra helps to remove discordant energies from your psychic energy field.

PADME—Literally, this translates into *"lotus."* It is a symbol of spiritual unfolding and the awakening of finer energies within your energy field. It has a sound that helps to
clarify the energy debris muddying your own energy field
and helps you sort out any problems you encountered during the day. It harmonizes your own psychic energy level.

HUM—This sound is untranslatable, per se. While OM represents the infinite sound within you and the universe, HUM
represents the finite within the infinite. It stands for the potential of the energy field, awakens your sensitivity to energies around you, and increases your awareness of how they
are affecting you. It awakens your perception of the physical
energy field and stimulates harmony within it so that you can
understand yourself more effectively as an energy system.

As in the first mantra, relax. Close your eyes, and as you inhale, sound the mantra silently to yourself. As you then exhale sound it audibly, projecting it outward, syllable by syllable. Find your own rhythm. Let it work for you. Know that as you use it your psychic energy field will become stronger and more protected at all times.

GENERAL RULES FOR STAYING ALIVE AND WELL AS A PSYCHIC BEING

To keep your intuition tools sharp, you must take care of them.

1. Practice protecting yourself in certain situations.

2. Maintain optimum health.

3. Practice exercises that work to cleanse and raise your energy level.

4. *To thine own self be true.* Treat others as you treat yourself. Live an honest life. Remember that what you do in life will come back to you. Positive energy comes back to you.

Because we can use our natural intuition in all areas of our lives, we need to look at its effects on our abilities in all areas of our lives and be constantly aware of how we are managing our overall energy.

CHAPTER 6

Advanced Tools: Meditation As a Pathway

MEDITATION IS BEING STILL

Meditation is emptying the self of all that hinders the creative forces from rising along the natural channels and being disseminated through those centers and sources that create the activities of the physical, the mental, and the spiritual person. The almost universal advice from spiritual teachers is this: If you want to become psychic gracefully, then allow your psychic abilities grow out of the practice of meditation. This process will involve letting go of old perceptions of yourself. It is the art of "dying to the world," letting go of your identification with your body and the physical world. Allow yourself to go to the "one place."

EXERCISE 37

A Simple Guide to Meditation

1. You will want to be in a quiet place. You may want to burn incense or play soft, calming music.

2. Close your eyes and relax. Notice that when you exhale your body relaxes.

3. Concentrate on your breathing and feel the relaxation with each exhalation.

4. With each inhalation concentrate on your oneness with your Creator or the Cosmos. Your mind will wander. Gently return your focus to breathing and oneness.

5. Continue breathing and focusing until you feel like a feather floating on a gentle breeze.

Let your breathing do the talking. This will have a dramatic affect on your attention and perception. The inner focus is repetitive, predictable, and boring—a kind of sensory deprivation, which actually increases the spiritual energies. When your consciousness is freed from sensation and attention, it can tune into itself. Once you are able to accomplish this, you will awaken your psychic awareness.

IMAGERY IN MEDITATION

I wanted to learn all I could about meditation because I wanted to feel close to my father after he died. When I meditate I visualize my father walking through a field of beautiful flowers. I meet him and embrace him with open arms, crying on his shoulders, laughing, smiling, spending time with him—on his plane, not mine— and saying farewells.

Eventually you can bring more and more purpose to meditation through imagery. Since sensory perception becomes highly attuned to spiritual and psychic levels, meditation can bring you to a state where almost anything is possible. Be careful what you concentrate on—you don't want to open your psychic centers in an unbalanced manner. Don't concentrate on a negative person or attribute. The imagination of the meditator is crucial in the creative patterning of psychic energies. Psychic forces stimulate the body's endocrine system, which has a unique pattern in every human being. When new energies enter our psychic centers, the pattern that is created must be healthy and positive. Our attention to this is necessary. Used correctly, meditation can open up the psychic centers to achieve a positive transformation of the body. Remember that meditation is a surrender to larger energies. There is will in surrender—the will to let go and let it happen. At the same time, we must choose wisely in willing what our purpose is as we go into another state.

The creative aspect of the mind determines the results of our meditating. We bring our traditions, assumptions, and expectations with us. As we become more aware of these things, we can let go and improve the quality of our experience. The soul forces will have an affect on the functioning of the body.

AVOIDING PROBLEMS

Breathing and meditating can sometimes open up the chakras unevenly. Energies may become focused where there is dis-ease. If you try to open specific chakras, this can lead to a crisis, best handled by a Spiritual Guide.

For the purpose of spiritual development—our goal here—it is better to open the chakra centers as an entire system. As you focus, hold in your mind a feeling of affirmation and allow it to resonate through your body to help you stay integrated.

Develop a purpose and pattern to your meditations. Allow the psychic energies to *circulate* within you for a graceful development of your abilities.

MEDITATION IS LIVING YOUR LIFE

Psychic energy should not be restricted to living only within your own body. It also needs to be allowed to circulate outwardly into your life. Sitting in silence is really only one-half of the meditation process. The other half is living the process. Meditation is a whole way of living. I feel that this is the hardest part to achieve because every day we are faced with decisions that we must deal with in a rational manner. But when we are not practiced at thinking clearly enough to avoid hurting another person, we can often overreact. Growing into the beneficial use of meditation takes time, just like learning how to walk.

From meditation we learn oneness and being in the world but not of it. Although both these attributes are developed in meditation, they need to be expressed during the day to complete the meditation cycle.

An ESP study showed how feelings of oneness arise during the practice of silent meditation. Meditating also increases your empathy for others. Empathy is a way of "being one with" another person. The feeling of being one with your Creator develops in the meditative state and can carry over to your waking life.

When we become one with life, feeling intimate with all we encounter, we may sense we need to protect everything, just the way we want to protect our individual, separate selves. This feeling can become a burden. Accepting responsibility for others as if they were a part of ourselves, yet not feeling the need to rescue them, is an attitude of detached concern. It combines caring with letting go. When we sit in meditation, our cares are expressed in our thoughts, yet we let them go. Meditation builds the capacity for detached concern.

Many psychics report traumatic experiences in childhood. A part of them became locked off in a safe, protected place away from the inner world. This is definitely true for me. I find that I often use the imagery of being under the wing of my Maker, protected and secure. You may have other imagery.

The inner child becomes the basis of psychic awareness when consciousness feels no boundaries with other people. Yet, wanting to make "everything right," the child psychic is burdened with the feelings of others. The danger of developing psychic ability without detached concern underlines the importance of meditation in making the transformation to a psychic awareness that is mature and able to develop further.

Once you become adept at meditation, you will experience the "cross-over" whereby you naturally go into meditative states when you need them—when you need to slow down or assess a situation more clearly. You psychic abilities will be more at your disposal, and your intuition will work more naturally in your life.

ACCEPTANCE IS THE KEY

Oneness is just a single example of the method and result of mediation, and it can serve as the ideal. Be one with the universe as it breathes through you. Test this out for yourself some starry night. Gaze up at the night sky and imagine you and the stars are the only things in existence. Don't think about letting the universe breathe through you or worry about doing it right, just do it.

Deep within all of us is the knowledge of and desire for meditation. The major stumbling block is always how to meditate or remembering how to do it. I have seen many people sit down to meditate with their brows wrinkled, trying to do it "right." I like the old expression: "It's as easy as falling off a log."

You should approach your meditation experience in the spirit of surrender and letting go. Place your attention on your breath and let your higher power do the rest. Remember, the most important things that happen in meditation are not the things that you do, but that are done to you through the psychic activity of the higher power. Accept meditation as a gift from your Creator. Behind all the descriptions I have given you and all the information you may receive from other psychics, the bottom line is that your psychic ability is a gift of creation. Accept the gift and more will be given—much more.

CHAPTER 7

Advanced Tools: Dreams As a Pathway

The dream is a little hidden door in the innermost secret recesses of the soul, opening into that cosmic night which was psyche long before there was any Ego-consciousness.

—CARL JUNG

THE HIDDEN DOORWAY

The chances are excellent that a dream will provide you with your first psychic experience. My interest in dreams began when I was a teenager. I dreamt of a robbery that happened near my home. I saw the robbery take place and I saw where the thief hid his stolen vehicle. When I told my Uncle Art, a policeman, about it, he knew better than to ask me how I knew about the robbery, which actually took place the same night I dreamt about it. I told him where the car was, and sure enough, it was exactly where I dreamt it would be. Amazing, isn't it?

Have you ever dreamt about a loved one had who passed away? Or would you like to dream of that person? All you have to do is sit back and ask your inner self, your intuitive self, to prepare for a visit with your loved one, and when you go to sleep you will dream of the visit with your deceased father, mother, spouse, sister, etc.

For me personally it is a relief to visit with my dear father in a dream. I am able to relieve the hurt of his leaving this Earth and visit with him in his world. Every dream is not so different than the first.

THE RELATIONSHIP OF DREAMS
TO PSYCHIC ABILITY

The most common—and the most useful—form of psychic ability you can develop is your dreams. It is no surprise to most people that your dreams can contain important information. There are stories from all over the world about dreams. The majority of reported psychic experiences involve dreams. Chances are if you have had any experience at all that makes you believe in the reality of psychic awareness, it came to you in a dream. You may have already had several psychic experiences in dreams without realizing it.

Sometimes people ask me to interpret dreams, and many times you can simply interpret the information contained in your own dream. Some people do not realize that there is a psychic message at all. Sometimes a dream sounds ordinary, other times not so ordinary, but the idea that it is psychic may not occur until later on. If you could produce a record of all of the dreams you have ever had, remembered or not, your own examination of these dreams would persuade you that you have had many psychic experiences.

PREMONITIONS

Nothing of significance has ever happened in our lives without our dreaming of it first. If you long to experience God's love and provision, it may be worth paying attention to your dreams. Sometimes our middle-of-the-night dreams offer uncommon guidance and wisdom, a direction for our lives that we might otherwise miss. Our dreams can even bring healing, a glimpse of the future, or an invitation to a deeper relationship with our maker.

There are many accounts of God speaking through dreams: Abraham, Jacob, Daniel, Solomon, and Joseph are just a few people from the Bible who were changed by dreams. Now, as then, God or the Higher Power is at work to calm our anxieties, heal our grief, or warn us of impending dangers. In our dreams, we can recognize our inner psychic self.

Perhaps dreaming of future events—precognitive dreaming—seems more far-fetched than telepathic dreaming, yet surveys have revealed that dreams about the future are much more common than telepathic dreams (telepathic dreaming is reading someone else's dreams while they sleep). Perhaps it is because dreams about the future have a greater chance of being proved while many telepathic dreams remain undetected.

One way to develop psychic awareness in your dreams is to be more observant of the process of falling asleep. When we sleep our sensitivity changes to a different level of vibration, a different frequency. In our sleeping state our psychic self emerges—as with the stars, which are always there but can't be seen because the sun is too bright.

A dreamer is really the soul and a dream is an experience of the soul. In the process of falling asleep, we die to our physical existence but awaken to our spiritual reality. Sleep is actually the "shadow" of death. In sleep as in death consciousness becomes unaware of the physical conditions surrounding the body, and there awakens a larger awareness that transcends time and space. The awakening of the "sixth sense," or psychic awareness, in sleep is a similar process. Why not try to make contact with this ability?

When falling asleep we become less aware in the normal sense. The mind of the physical body is shutting down. You most likely have experienced this already when drifting off to sleep in front of your television or when someone was reading aloud. Suddenly you realized that you haven't been hearing what was going on but were in a world of your own. Your conscious mind was going to sleep, and you were awakening to your subconscious mind.

When I want to wake up at 8 A.M., I tell my mind before I go to sleep. I fall asleep and I awaken at exactly 8 A.M. I feel the subconscious and the conscious work together. When your conscious mind is shutting down, its response to the most physical kind of information, like when to wake up, is simultaneously opening up information from the imagination to the subconscious mind. We exchange waking reality for dreaming reality.

Sometimes when we are falling asleep, we hear voices and experience unusual changes in the perception of the body; these are commonplace in this twilight zone. As we continue to fall asleep, our senses undergo a change. Hearing, for example, becomes activated throughout the body.

"Listen to what your body is trying to tell you." Have you ever heard that advice? It is a suggestion to pay attention to subtle clues from your body. The subconscious mind does just that during sleep. It operates not just through the brain, but through the nervous system. That is why we often have dreams about the condition of our body or the bodies of those close to us. Sometimes we have dreams about circumstances in other people's lives, and in this case we should listen to our dreams as they are telling us something.

If you dream of numbers, play them in the lottery. If you dream someone in your family is going to have a baby, she most likely will. If you dream about someone dying, the person you dreamed about has failing health. If you dream that someone has an accident, warn that person to be careful when going on a trip. If you dream about falling and you reach the ground, it is said you will never wake up. I hope you never reach the ground.

Such awareness during sleep is listening with our "third ear," which is our "sixth sense" or psychic ability. It is a form of ESP. In sleep, as our awareness diffuses throughout the body, we awaken to our psychic awareness. Dreams are one of the experiences of this sixth sense!

A DREAMER IS THE SOUL

What does the soul do when it dreams? The soul has universal awareness, which includes its memories from experiences in past lives, particular lessons learned. (See my book *How to Discover Your Past Lives.*) The soul, possessing wisdom from a multitude of experiences, brings that perspective to bear as it reviews events and activities of the day. This evaluation of a day of life from the overall perspective of several lifetimes is somewhat like the judgment parents make about events in the life of their child. The child's own activities may appear ironic, humorous, sad, or hopeful when viewed from the wider perspective of the adult.

THE PURPOSE OF DREAMING

The purpose of our dreams is guidance. Just as a parent evaluates the behavior of a child from an adult perspective, the soul examines the person's experiences from the viewpoint of lifetimes of learning. It is this evaluation that is the dream and the purpose of that dream—one of the main ways our soul has of guiding us.

How are we doing? What are we doing? Where we are headed is compared with where we really want to go, how we really want to be. Dreams are experiences of discovery, when we see from the soul's point of view what our daily experiences mean to us. You could say it is the comparison of ideal and the real.

So how does this guidance function and what can it do for us? The soul's experience (or the perception of the dream) during the dreaming state remains with us after we dream. Even if we can't remember the dream, we are remembering our soul's experience of discovery. We may recall it as a strange experience or a nightmare because it does not seem real to us. When we have nightmares, it is the soul's way of telling us of a past experience that was a bad one.

REMEMBERING DREAMS

If you have trouble remembering your dreams, you are not alone. As soon as you wake up, try to remember your dream. Lie very still and examine how you feel and what you are thinking. Place a pad of paper near your bed and when you wake up jot down what you remember about your dream. If you dreamt of any numbers, write them down before you fall back to sleep. Chances are when you fall back to sleep and you awaken, you will not remember your dream.

You may want to keep a dream journal to develop your psychic awareness. Get in the habit of writing down your dreams. Not only will this exercise persuade your unconscious that you value your dreams, but it will help you appreciate the psychic dimension of dreams.

The most common form of psychic experience in dreams is about the future. When I was younger I kept a dream journal for several years along with my personal diary. Later I went back and examined the two diaries and found many examples where both contained an image that appeared later on in my life.

It is just as likely for an image in a dream to be based upon an experience in the past as upon an experience in the future! Sometimes my own dreams are about experiences I have had at one time or another. These experiences and dreams fluctuate through my life at different times.

Another level of attunement is to relive the dream itself in your imagination, letting the feeling in the dream seep in. Your dream will accomplish the goals you have set for yourself. Attune your psychic awareness so your dreams will follow through for you. You will then be able to feel your dream's vibrations so that the meaning of your dream is transferred to you.

Dreams can take us into whatever region of life we wish to explore, provided that during the day we are making efforts in that direction. "As awake, so asleep, it's what's on your mind that counts!"

EVALUATING YOUR DREAMS

Since your first psychic experience might very well occur in a dream, don't miss out on that opportunity to develop your ability. During the day ask yourself if you are prepared to remember your next dream whether it is good or bad. As you fall asleep that night imagine yourself waking up in the morning with a helpful dream. Then record your thoughts and impressions upon awakening. Note the setting of your dream, the characters and time frame, and the narrative structure—the beginning, middle, and end.

During the day look for patterns of correspondence between your dreams, waking impressions, and the day's experiences. Don't be too rational about evaluating any perceived correspondences. If you sense a link, assume there is one. The correspondences you find are opportunities to apply your psychic abilities.

Ask yourself if there are messages in your dreams that you should pay attention to. To think or meditate about the specific dream you had, I suggest you sit quietly and make your dream the mantra or focus of meditation.

EXERCISE 38

Evaluating a Dream

1. Begin your process of meditation (see Exercise 37 in chapter 6, "Advanced Tools: Meditation as a Pathway").

2. Read your dream aloud from your dream journal or notes.

3. As you hear your dream in the meditative state, all sorts of novel ideas about the meaning of the dream will appear spontaneously.

4. Speak aloud any ideas that come to you.

5. After the meditation, write down the ideas and look for correspondences. Keep with your dream journal and refer to it as events unfold.

Here is an example from my own life. Before I went to visit my daughter in North Carolina, I dreamed that I was playing with children and visiting a new church. When I arrived in North Carolina I went to the Marine base where my daughter lived, but my son-in-law wouldn't let me stay with them. I walked to a Dairy Queen, sat down, and contemplated what I was going to do next. I didn't know anyone except my daughter. I began to meditate. Soon I met a woman whose husband was stationed in another country, and I told her my dilemma. She offered to let me stay in her house if I would watch her little boy while she went to work. I took her up on her offer, baby-sat her son, and got a roof over my head. This woman took me to her church, where I met people who took up a collection for me so I could fly home.

MAKING FRIENDS
WITH YOUR DREAM LIFE

You can have many different relationships with your dream life or no relationship at all. But if you decide to have a positive relationship with your dreams, your life will be richer. You will be more psychic and reap the benefits of allowing more of your intuitive self into your life. Your sense of self will expand, and your identity will be more about who you really are.

GENERAL TIPS ABOUT DREAMS

1. If a dream strikes you as particularly important, write it down as soon as you wake up or else you may forget it. Unless you have been in the habit of ignoring your dreams, you will probably know when a dream is significant.

2. Our dreams are always right about what we are feeling, but they are not necessarily objectively true. For instance, you may have a dream that someone you love is killed in an accident. That person may live a long time, but the dream may be a forewarning for that person about driving in bad weather. Sometimes this dream means that there will be a birth in that family.

3. It certainly does matter what we do with our dreams. If God or the universe or our own soul is speaking to us through our dreams, we should respond.

4. Dreams tell us stories through symbols. Unlike signs, which are one-dimensional, symbols are multidimensional. Symbols are familiar objects, people, or words that take on a larger meaning in our dreams. If you dream you are racing cars, your dream may be telling you that you are driving recklessly or that you are acting irresponsibly. It may be warning you to slow down so you can decide your own fate.

5. Dreams have multiple functions: spiritual, psychological, and psychic. Some of our dreams help us to review, recognize, and comment on the day's events.

6. Most dreams tell a story in which you are the main character. Strange as it may sound, you can also be many characters in your dream. You can dream yourself in another time or place, and who knows, maybe you were there. You can discover many interesting things about yourself, things you don't feel comfortable with in your waking hours.

7. Pay attention to how your dream makes you feel. Are you sad, frightened, astonished, happy, peaceful, embarrassed?

8. Everyone dreams in color, whether we remember or not. The colors themselves may have meaning.

9. Dreams of falling are common, but in these we never seem to hit the ground. If we were to hit the ground, we would die.

10. A nightmare is a dream of our fears. It is an alarm whose purpose is to "wake us up" to something we need to face.

Every evening, millions of people lie down to sleep not suspecting they will soon take center stage in dramas of their own creating. As we develop our psychic skills, we will automatically use our dreams for benefit in our own lives and the lives of others. You can even consciously direct the subject of your dreams by instructing yourself to dream of something.

Dreams may also be a glimpse of the future that offers guidance, brings healing, provides wisdom, and beckons us to a deeper relationship with the One who made us dreamers in the first place.

Here is the dream of the wise King Solomon. Young Solomon inherited the throne of Israel from his father David. One night, after worshipping God, Solomon was given a dream that transformed his life. In the dream, God appeared and told Solomon to ask for whatever he wanted. With surprising humility Solomon replied, "I am an only child and don't know how to carry out my duties. Your servant is here among the people you have chosen, a great people, too numerous to count or number. So give your servant a discerning heart to govern your people and to distinguish between right and wrong." Pleased that Solomon hadn't asked for long life, riches, or the death of his enemies, God responded, "I will do what you have asked. I will give you a wise and discerning heart so that there will never have been anyone like you, nor will there ever be." Blessed be the man who knew the value of wisdom and knew it to be a gift.

Another example is that of Albert Einstein who in his adolescence had a dream to which he traced his understanding of relativity. In the dream he was riding a sled that kept going faster, accelerating until it approached the speed of light. The stars began to take on new patterns and colors, dazzling the boy on the sled. Einstein commented that his entire career could be seen as an extended meditation on that dream.

Surely if dreams can inspire great music, science, literature, provide solutions to mathematical problems, and even result in an improved golf swing, they can occasionally offer help in resolving personal dilemmas for which wisdom is needed. We are a people starved for the spiritual and psychic side of what is beyond chance. As never before, we hear of angels, dreams, visions, apparitions, and miracles. Many of us are no longer in danger of scorning the supernatural. Rather, we are in danger of embracing every claim to supernatural experience that confronts us without discerning its source. The best chance we have against confusion is good old rationalism—what we can see, feel, smell, touch, hear, or intuitively read with our psychic abilities.

Because of a dream . . . many people are forewarned about disasters.

Because of a dream . . . ordinary people are guided in extraordinary ways.

Because of a dream . . . came the Book of Revelation.

PART

III

THE MEANING OF PSYCHIC AWARENESS

CHAPTER

8

Psychic Energy
in the World

Applying your psychic awareness in the world is something you do when you have accepted this part of yourself. Your creativity in all activities will unfold as you allow your whole being to participate in life. In this chapter there are stories that may inspire you from my own life and the lives of my clients.

SIMPLE PSYCHIC AWARENESS

There are many of us who are aware of being psychic—only we are in denial at times. Then we may be slapped in the face by our awareness of even a minute slice of our psychic energy. Helen is a friend and associate who insisted there is no such thing as a "true psychic." She came to her opinion because of the 900-number telephone hot lines for psychics who want you to call them to hear about your past and future. A true psychic can pick up on your energies and tell you things without your telling them anything at all, but

Helen had decided that psychic incidents were all coincidence or fate. Her own psychic awareness kicked in, however, in an emergency situation. She was about to cross railroad tracks at a crossing whose gate was broken. She did not know the gate was broken, but something told her not to cross the tracks. She got out of her car and looked down the tracks. What did she see—an oncoming freight train two hundred feet away. If her intuitive self hadn't questioned her or nudged her to check out the gate, she wouldn't be here now talking about her newly developed psychic awareness.

PRECOGNITION

This is a very special story about someone close to me—my father who is now deceased. He was cognitive about many things before they happened. Being an Italian who grew up in the city, he was also street smart and cautious. His favorite saying was, "If it sounds too good to be true, it probably is." I think many of us feel this way, even if we don't come from the old school of hard knocks.

When I was a small girl, my father was cleaning out an old gas tank. Knowing that it was about five years old, he didn't think any harm could come from cleaning it. It took him a few evenings, and on the third night when he went to bed, he dreamt that the tank blew up while he was standing next to it. The next evening as he was finishing cleaning the tank, he suddenly rushed into the house and told us all to go to someplace safe. My mother thought he was crazy, but as we all stood huddled in the basement, there was a loud explosion in the driveway. It was the gas tank. If my father hadn't paid heed to his dream, he would have been blown up. When we asked him how he knew things before they happened, he would say, "That's my secret." But my mom and I knew.

It is hard to tell you when I first had psychic experiences. I have been having them for as long as I can remember. The ones I hate are those that tell me someone is going to die. I know who and the exact date and time. I tend to argue with the psychic in me, because I dislike hearing these things. However, it is energy I am picking up on. They can be as far away as Africa.

There was a time I was going to visit my daughter at school on her lunch hour. On the way I pulled over to the side of the road without even thinking about it. In front of me, I watched a four-car pileup. It was awful. A car rammed into a telephone pole, and I watched it bend and break in half, falling on two oncoming cars. I saw a truck ram into the car that hit the pole. I sat in my car and watched the whole horrible thing. A cop asked me, "Why did you pull over?" I told him, "I don't know. I just did."

When I was around twelve in Allendale, New Jersey, a bank robber escaped from the Hackensack police and came up to Allendale. My grandmother lived next to an underpass, and I walked through it at lunchtime to get from school to her house. She called my mother to tell her that I would be going through the underpass with an escaped bank robber in the area and that she was not able to warn me. As I entered the first steps down into the long, cold hallway that led to the other side of town, I stopped. I listened and heard nothing out of the ordinary, but something kept telling me not to enter the underpass. I walked through this underpass every day, to and from school, and on my lunch hour. But suddenly I just was not going to do any walking in the underpass. I didn't know what to do. I just stood there. Within a few minutes, which seemed like hours to me, the police pulled up and rushed past me as if I wasn't there. Then they walked out of the underpass with a man in handcuffs. I continued on to my grandmother's house, where she called my mother to say that I was all right. It's funny that she didn't know that I stopped on the steps and funny that the cops didn't seem to see me standing there. It was almost as if I had been invisible.

Another time, there was a bank robbery in Allendale, where I lived most of my life until I got married. It was believed that the bank robbers hid the money someplace on the old trolley tracks. Everyone and his brother were looking for that bag of money. My house was in front of the trolley tracks and my cousin Art and I used to ride our bikes on the tracks. We were told not to do so until the thieves were caught, but we never paid any attention to our parents. I told my cousin that the money was hidden in a tree where he and I used to climb and had notched our names. It was an old oak next to a stream where we used to fish. He looked at me like I was crazy, but he knew better than to shrug me off. We rode our bikes to the tree and in the hollow of the trunk there was the bag of money. Can you imagine what went through our minds—it was so exciting. We got our reward of about $200, which we split and spent on new bikes. Still, we were scolded because we hadn't listened to our parents about not going on those old trolley tracks.

My last precognition story is a sad one, and it came from a dream. The dream told me about my cousin Art dying in a bad car accident. I saw how the car he was riding in hit a tree and killed him instantly, and how he was with God, how he missed me, and how much he loved me. The dream told me what the car looked like and where the accident happened. It showed me his bloody clothes and shoes. I woke up crying hysterically. My mother came into my room and asked what was wrong. I cried and told her. Ten minutes later the phone rang. It was my uncle telling my mother that his son had just been killed in a car accident. That night, as we tried to get back to sleep, my mother held me close and we cried together. My cousin appeared to us and said, "I just came to say goodbye."

PSYCHIC ENERGY AND PLANTS

Naturally, psychic energy is not just available to humans. Plants can also benefit from it and enjoy receiving it and feeling its flow.

Since plants come in a variety of sizes, from a few millimeters (seeds) to several hundred feet (sequoias), different periods of time are required for treating them with your psychic energy. Two or three minutes for seeds and five to ten minutes for room plants have been found to be effective periods of time.

If we wish to supply large plants or a small garden with psychic energy, the easiest way is to charge the water we are giving them. In my experience one or two minutes per quart is sufficient. Whether the charge is sufficient or not can easily be tested with a pendulum, as discussed in chapter 2, "Tools of the Psychic Trade." If the pendulum provides no evidence of negative vibrations, the water can be used.

You should always treat the roots of houseplants, not just the leaves. If transmitted to the roots, psychic energy will be a remedy for soft rot, whether for prevention or healing. Regular transferal of your energy to the root system encourages freshly potted plants to spread their roots in the new soil and adapt to their new environment.

Pests

If plants are infested by pests, you can effectively help them with your life force energy. A few minutes of transferring your energies will be sufficient to increase the vitality of houseplants so they are able to form enough resistance to parasites. As a rule, the pests will have dropped off the plant by the next day. However, since parasites pass on poisonous substances into the earth, thereby continuing to affect the plant even after their removal, we should wash the leaves thoroughly. Apply some more energy from the palms of your hands over the next few days to revitalize the plant. This is very important, as it might otherwise not stand the strain of the defensive reaction, especially in the case of abundant infestation.

Trees

Trees act as wonderful companions for meditation. Stand close to a strong tree and place your palms on its trunk or embrace it. After a while you will sense its powerful, calm presence. During this process you give it your energy and the tree takes you into its own energy field. If you do this regularly with a particular tree, it may reveal images or other impressions. Trees can be good advisors if they trust you. If you now think I've slightly gone mad, just try it— you will be as surprised as I was when I first made contact with a tree.

Acid Rain

In this day and age, it is very important that we humans do not use the world like a self-service shop, with a "just throw it away, tomorrow the shelves will be refilled" attitude. This attitude has already caused immeasurable damage. If you have been concentrating on the exercises in this book and almost perfected them, you can do a lot to help trees live (and survive). Find out which particular forests near your home are especially damaged and send them regular energy via distance treatment. It would be even better if you were joined by a group of friends who could also channel their combined energy to this forest or tree. This kind of tree support group is often able to accomplish small miracles. If you are interested in environmental work with your psychic energy, please drop me a note, in care of the publisher. I will collect the addresses and pass them on to interested people (only if you grant your consent of course). If you have some experience with this kind of application, (transferring healing energies), I would appreciate it if you could share it with me. It may prove to be useful to an environmental network and for good use to the world.

PSYCHIC ENERGY AND ANIMALS

All animals love to feel the transfer of energy. They are very sensitive to psychic energy and know exactly how much and at which part of the body they need it. In other words, it is they who determine the duration and the priorities of transferring your psychic energy to them.

This is how a psychic energy session with an animal can typically take place: You are having a cup of tea with a friend. Suddenly, your dog or cat comes up to you, prods you with its nose and leans against you. If you place your hands on the animal, it will position itself so that the right spot is touched. Once the animal gets restless or goes away, the session is over.

Recently my mother's dog, Auggie, felt terribly sick due to arthritis. He is an old dog who loves the outside and just won't come in even if there is a hurricane. Now he wouldn't eat or come in the house to keep warm. I went up to him and placed my arms around his neck as if I were giving him a long, lasting hug. I released all my psychic energy into him, using the tornado exercise (see Exercise 34 in chapter 5, "Strengthening Your Psychic Energy Field"). Energy spiraled from the top of my head right into the dog's body and out into the earth. Within a few minutes, he was back chasing the ball I threw to him. Later, he cuddled up in my arms, waiting for more hugs, but this time it was for attention and love, not healing.

Such transfer-of-energy sessions will affect your relationship to the animal concerned; I have seen true friendships develop as a result of these energy treatments. The animals lose their natural shyness and become very trusting.

Large or dangerous animals should be provided healings only with distant energies. If that is not possible, you can at least charge their food and drinking water with your energy. The effect is less than that of direct energy treatment, but if done regularly over a long period of time, this will also be of help. As for the food, domestic animals are normally given factory-produced food and tap water. Neither is ideal for their well-being. If it is not possible to provide healthier food such as fresh meat and or spring water, you can at least charge the food with your energy. Place the palms of your hands on their food and transfer your energy by channeling through the chakra vessels. This reduces the effect of harmful substances and the food is more easily digested. Incidentally, the same is also true for your own food.

Horses

I have learned from a veterinary practitioner of natural therapeutics that he cures horses of troublesome colic much faster by using his psychic energy. If our psychic energy is given along with a homeopathic remedy, there is often an improvement within a half an hour. Simply place the palms of your hands on the horse's stomach. After a while change to another area of the horse.

Dogs, Again

My mother's dog, Auggie, was very sick. He had a deer tick on his body, which caused a fever of 105°. I placed my hands on his head and directed my energy toward him. Within an hour he was up to his old self, running after a ball and chasing and catching for anyone who would pay attention to him. As for me, I was sick for two days with a fever.

Cats

Castration is almost inevitable for domestic cats. Cats are often sterilized so that they aren't constantly in heat and suffer accordingly (of course this is also done to control the population). By transferring your psychic energy you will be able to help your feline companions cope with the operation and shorten the period of convalescence. Cats in heat become more peaceful if they receive a lot of energy during this time. It also helps if you chant the vowel "ooooo" or "OM" from the depths of your stomach. The vibration of this chant corresponds to the sexual center and gets the animal in touch with the energy it desires. But it works only if the sound is really formed in your stomach; if it isn't, the vibration of the second chakra will be missing. If your friends think you are crazy when you intone a deep abdominal "OM," don't worry. They will get used to it. Perhaps they will even adopt the method after seeing that it works.

Basically, psychic energy has its effect on all beings in your environment. Plants and animals will feel good in your presence and encounter you with greater trust. Your hand chakras are constantly passing your life force energies into your orbital cycle, and therefore whatever comes into contact with your energy field also comes in contact with those innate energies. You may notice that your hands start to tingle when you are near certain animals or plants. (And this won't be an allergic reaction either.) This simply means that they are absorbing a dose of life energy from you.

It may well be that your pet will be a little confused by your energy. It can feel the change in your vibrations and is unable to understand it at first. It will soon come up to you and will be snuggling in your hands.

You will also notice that animals in particular can sense spiritual happenings before they happen or can actually see a ghost or spiritual entity. This is because an animal's energy level is so high in their sensitivity area—their eyes, ears, and sense of smell—that they can easily detect something that we ordinarily overlook.

INSPIRATION

A simple spontaneous experience can inspire and nurture us for a long time.

When my father died, I hated to hear the word God. When people came to the house and started to preach about God, I would slam the door in their face, and I would curse God. After all, my father was prayed for and he died anyway. What the hell? My father was always looking for the cure he never got for his stroke and heart condition.

It wasn't until I spoke directly to my guardian angel that I knew the miracle my father was looking for was given to me. There was a reason my Dad died; it was his time. Even though I thought it was unfair that God took away the man I adored all my life, the miracle that my father could have had and never did get was given to me. Maybe it was given to me so that I could tell everyone about the love that God revealed to me in the five years following my cancer-free stage. Maybe God knew I would be a good soldier for Him.

I will never forget the woman who stayed with me during and after my surgery . I told her, "You're my guardian angel, aren't you?"

"You're going to be fine and live to be ninety-nine years old. You won't see me anymore," she said and walked out of my room. No one else saw her. But I knew she was my guardian angel. These angels are there to help us in transitions in life and in transitions from our world to the spiritual world.

✹

CHAPTER

9

Spiritual Dimensions

I wish for all of you to hold steady in the awareness of your psychic abilities as you find a greater soul inside of you, the great "I AM." To discern the full circle of your soul's mind from the endless patterns of your creative imagination within to the endless reflections of the divine mind in all creation is an ability that is universal. The "here and now" mind of ordinary experiences is potentially infinite, and if we get quieter still, we can shift to the subconscious and allow ourselves to be sensitive to its subtle promptings and new dimensions of infinite scope are within our reach.

THE BODY REFLECTS THE SOUL

Your sixth sense should be developing well by now. And I expect you feel it as a natural part of yourself and even believe that it is probably accessible to all. The container for all this energy is the body, and we must continue to be aware of its care and feeding.

The body is like an historical artifact that signals to those who can see a clue to the nature of the originator. The body is the physical residue of the soul's expression, because the vibrational energy of the soul has been patterned by images created in the mind. As materiality hypnotized souls, they developed bodies and became "trapped" in them. Yet the body is not simply the symptom of this hypnotic entanglement; it is also the symbol of what has become entrapped. The body thus has a correspondence with the soul and points to it. The body, in other words, is like a physical image of the soul, as that which was created in the image of the Creator.

Correspondence has many dimensions. For example, you can read a person's feelings from how the body expresses itself through posture. Our posture reflects our moods. A sad person may stoop or slouch; a happy person may walk tall. Handwriting is another typical expression of the inner person, as many graphologists will tell you. When you develop your psychic abilities to a fuller extent, you will be able to read another person's body by observing the way they walk, talk, or, most importantly, by looking into their eyes.

Speaking of soul, did you know that your soul is three-dimensional? It consists of body, mind, and spirit. We "earthlings" generally compare the oneness of ourselves to the trinity, or the three forms of the soul. In the unity, the soul expresses itself, and each of the three forms corresponds to a different level of mind. The superconscious mind expresses itself in the form of the soul body (which is also called the spirit body), the energy body, and the casual body. The subconscious mind expresses itself in the form of the astral body. The conscious mind expresses itself in the form of the physical body. The two nonphysical bodies, which connote gaseous, near invisible, etheric bodies, are another level of reality.

THE DIMENSIONS OF SOUL
Soul Body

Soul is the purest, highest, or most basic form of being. Soul is energy, a pattern in final form. It is our energy body. This soul body is where we can discern our true psychic energies. The other bodies—physical, etheric, and astral—are not our essence. Think of it this way: We can burn a book, but we can't burn away the ideas in that book, for the ideas are more real than the book. In much the same way, the physical body can be destroyed, but soul body is never destroyed. Likewise, the etheric and astral bodies cannot be destroyed.

Etheric Body

The etheric body is what I have been referring to as the energy field around the body and is contained within our energy level of psychic awareness.

Mental/Astral Body

The mental or astral body is the second level of reality, which is that of patterns. It may also be called the dream body because dreams often reflect mental patterns that are about to manifest physically.

Physical Body

The subconscious mind and the mental/astral body functions are reflected in the physical body through the autonomic nervous system. The conscious mind and the physical body are reflected by and operate through the cerebral-spinal system.

This system includes the sensory system and the voluntary nervous system, which control our muscles. To the average person this system pretty much defines the real world, along with the sensory-material world that we can interact with consciously.

When we look at the physical body in a traditional way, the subconscious mind makes for a very strange bedfellow. The linkage between to the two, however, is crucial to our understanding of the nature of psychic energies and how our conscious and subconscious minds can influence the operation of these energies.

PATHS TO THE SOUL

I would like to repeat what I said in Chapter 1. The ancient Greek advice "Know thyself" is a good suggestion for developing your psychic ability.

To know thyself exacts a price, it also offers a reward.
The price is that we must bear the burden of responsibility
for that which we are. We can't blame others for what
we make ourselves into, and our reward is found in
self-acceptance and the freedom to be who we are.

Near-Death and Past-Life Experiences

It is no accident that the various techniques used for recalling past lives evoke reactions similar to those obtained in the recollection of childhood memories in psychotherapy. There is fear and reluctance, and these are blocks. By working through these resistances, reliving past experiences, accepting our role in these events, incorporating them into our personal histories, and feeling forgiveness and acceptance, these processes lead to a sense of relief, peace of mind, and freedom. There is also an expansion of self-concept, as our conscious identity now includes all that we had forgotten, and our history falls into place as a coherent pattern of meaning. Creative energy is released and enables us to live life more fully.

Psychic ability is a function of the soul's experience during many lifetimes. In a reading concerning the development of my own psychic abilities, I learned I was once a nun, but I was wounded by people throwing stones at me. I prayed at that time to be released from all the pain my body was in, and I had an out-of-body experience. This learning has carried me over into the life of clairvoyance and developing my psychic abilities. Another life as a librarian has given me my specialty, writing.

There are a number of routes to the transformation of personality that have often been termed "coming home," recognizing and returning to the roots of one's true nature. A near-death experience can have that effect; depth psychotherapy can have that effect; and so can the development of psychic awareness, when constructively applied.

A near-death experience that increases psychic abilities also awakens the realization of the reality of our soul. A person so affected becomes less worried about death and self-preservation and values love relationships more. It is interesting, too, that people who have had a near-death experience often see the memories of their lives played out for them. Furthermore, people who have been psychoanalyzed continually "free associate." These people no longer hide from themselves and they exhibit qualities that are the fruits of long-term, depth psychotherapy. I have studied this through a dear friend of mine who hypnotizes people into regressing into their past lives. Some of the experiences we have in our lifetime today reflect the same patterns experienced in another lifetime.

Of these paths to the soul, you can develop your psychic awareness in the context of spiritual growth. Taking one step at a time, you have been developing this psychic awareness while working with this book. The next step is to "know thyself." Learning how to develop your psychic ability can occur with the help of a loving family or friends who will provide support and honest feedback. Next, I suggest meditating to allow the mind and body to become one and to be receptive to the soul's vibrations. I also value prayer, to direct attention back to God, as well as to help others in time of need. Then, find a way to put your energies and talents to use helping others, especially the talents that emerge in the form of psychic abilities.

Pathway to the Soul

Step 1   Develop psychic awareness, and practice this awareness.

Step 2   Know thyself through therapy, honest relationships, etc.

Step 3   Practice meditation/prayer.

Step 4   Use your talents for the benefit of others.

Psychic abilities are a function of knowledge and skills that are developed and constructively applied. What we use is ours to keep. I encourage you to take a practical approach in developing your innate psychic abilities. We should look for our psychic abilities when they first appear in those areas of our life where some creative talent is already being used in service to others and go from there. I consider this to be one part self-development at the spiritual, mental, and physical levels; one part service to others, at the level of prayer and the practical level of everyday interactions with others. In this way, one step at a time, balanced development is assured. Psychic abilities are not some new superhuman power, but the natural expression of your soul, created in the image of your Creator.

HOW TO CHANNEL YOUR HIGHER SELF

Try meditating and invite your inner self to join you in silence. Whether through meditation, prayer, or the sending of telepathic suggestions while you are in a relaxed state, you may find your higher self appearing. There is also the added benefit of a more peaceful sleep!

Using an altered state of consciousness to elicit imagery for creative problem solving is a good application for learning to channel your higher self. Think more about channeling than about any of the other exercises in this book. Once you have mastered the trance state, enter it with a specific question. (You can also enter this state of mind when you are hypnotized.) Having asked your questions, allow your mind to run freely. Be aware of thoughts that may whisper to you. Accept any feeling of knowing that they may exist. Be sensitive to the images that may arise. Very often a solution comes in the dream of a single image rather than all at once. That single image can be the intuition of your higher self speaking in a very succinct manner.

The same method can be used for interpreting dreams. While in this trance state, have a friend read one of your dreams aloud to you. Then call upon the highest power within you and allow yourself to speak about your dream. I have found that even amateurs can deliver quite a meaningful discourse about their own dreams in this manner. Deep within all of us we know the truth about ourselves. If we are willing to assume responsibility for consciously knowing the truth, we can use this method to bring that knowledge into awareness. For this purpose, the trance state itself may prove to be less important than the attitude of acceptance.

SAINTLINESS AND ESP

In the ancient yoga tradition it was common knowledge that psychic powers developed as a result of intense meditation with our Creator. The same holds true in Western mysticism. I surveyed biographies of saints and found that 30 percent of them exhibited ESP. For instance, they came to a person's aid (appearing in two places at once) and they acquired knowledge clairvoyantly. The majority of these saints were not born psychic, but their skills increased with their spiritual work and progress. There is something very special or important about these spiritual saints who exhibit psi phenomena. When you let go of the concerns of the world, your psychic abilities seem to become more pronounced. I know it is hard not to exhibit emotions other than the ones we have been trained to ever since we were born. It is hard for me to let go of emotions that aren't good for me or the person on the receiving end of them. I have to come to an understanding of my relationship with my Creator and what He would want me to do, even though I can't understand why.

Spirituality seems to have more to do with being smart, as in enlightened, rather than being good, as in perfect. The only connection I feel we have in life is the oneness we have with our creator. The essence of love, of service to others— in effect the essence of transcendence—is to act on the basis of a perception of oneness, of an interdependent whole. That seems to be the emerging meaning of spirituality. I view this relationship of psychic awareness to spirituality in that same oneness. Psychic abilities, including those of prophecy, exist because in reality we are souls: interconnected miniature versions of the whole creation, holographic atoms of the body of God. Does that mean that when we are imperfect our Creator is, too?

That is a very difficult question in a sense, and how would one answer it? I feel that when we came into this world as a soul, we were perfect. And everything in our life that molded us to what we are today and the negative energies around us that have affected our life are like diseases. These negative energies infiltrate our perfect soul structure, to make us imperfect. It is only through reacquainting ourselves to what we lost that we can achieve a restoration to our perfection. That seems to be the emerging meaning of spirituality. When we attempt to use our psychic energies for personal gain I believe we fall short of what is expected from us by our Creator. We just miss that mark and that constricts our focus of the self. Psychic ability is an expression of the whole. It is designed to be used for the betterment of the whole, including, if necessary, improving our recognition and application of our unique contribution to humanity.

Psychic abilities in us can be seen both as an outgrowth and a means of attuning to a higher pattern of being. These abilities are the pattern of an individual in a conscious, creative, and responsible relationship to all humanity.

YOUR SPIRITUAL PATH

Psychic energy plays a vital part in the process of respiritualizing mankind that will give our lives value and meaning.

Every part of the psychic's abilities reconnects everyone and everything back to the Earth and stars. It reopens our psychic abilities, which for many years have been forgotten. Learning the nature of our psychic abilities—what they are, and how and why they happen—is a learning process of the life force within us.

Developing our innate psychic energy is the key to transmitting health to every living creature on Earth. Working with the psychic energy/life force of the human body can be almost effortless and simple. This knowledge has a spiritual urgency for us now.

CHAPTER

10

Continuing on Your Way

YOUR NEW EXPANDING SELF

Don't take anybody's word for it. Try it for yourself and see. Do the exercises. Keep a journal. You'll learn more secrets by your own experiments and practice than just by thinking about them. Besides, only the ideas that actually work for you, those you use and that make a difference in your life, are worth anything anyway. Enlightenment doesn't come by sitting quietly waiting for the good fairy to sprinkle pixie dust over you, but by enlightened action that bears the fruit of knowledge.

What kind of enlightenment action have you taken since reading this book? Be honest. Have you followed specific instructions or suggestions given in the preceding chapters? You may wish to try some additional experiences during your own adventure into the world of psychic awareness.

By now you have learned that you are one with the world. By now you may *believe* in the possibility of ESP, which helps develop psychic ability. Allow your imagination to embrace the concepts that transcend space, time, and the cause-and-effect chain of atomistic thinking. Imagine ideas as permeating the fourth dimension and allow your own mind to become a sympathetic resonator to these patterns. Imagine that behind the veil of your conscious awareness there exists a superconscious intelligent awareness. Develop your own image of this intelligence at work, this Ancient One within you who is guiding you at this very moment in your next step in awakening the innate psychic energy within you.

SET ASIDE TIME
FOR YOURSELF

How many times have you heard this? I hear it all the time. You may not be ready to begin a program of meditation even though you are aware of its supreme value in developing your psychic abilities. That's perfectly okay. Applying your innate intuitive abilities before you begin any special program of development is a natural way to proceed. Regular meditation is a special mode of learning to set aside the conscious mind in favor of superconscious awareness, but there are other ways to practice the art of letting go.

This is an exercise similar to what is called in the Eastern tradition "mindfulness meditation." You can use it as an aid to work with spontaneous intuition. For brief periods of time, then for longer periods, try to stay in contact with your background awareness, then simply "step aside" and watch yourself go by. That is without interfering with or changing any of your thoughts and actions—simply observe them. At first, you may wish to practice repeating the phrase, "Now, I am aware that I *am* . . . thinking about this or doing that," and so forth. The idea is to be able to combine awareness with spontaneity. We usually are able to have one or the other, but not both at the same time.

Practicing this form of ongoing meditation will yield several useful benefits.You will learn self-acceptance by this exercise. You may become aware of "Now I am blocking out feelings about. . . ." Or, "Now, I am criticizing myself for. . . ." Self-criticism inhibits curiosity and has the effect of closing you down rather than opening you to spontaneity.

As you practice this form of awareness, you can take an inventory of habitual thought patterns that interfere with the development of higher consciousness. Do you find that you are skeptical of developing psychic abilities? Do you have patterns of worry, fear, or anger? Make a note of them. Later you can investigate these patterns to see how you might work with them and not against them.

Use inspirational writing to have a dialogue between the insecure you and your higher self. By taking an attentive, loving interest in those parts of yourself that you want to change, you will break the fruitless habit of thoughtless, automatic self-criticism and learn to recognize the various needs that these parts are trying to bring to your attention.

Accepting your knee-jerk perfectionism and underlying fears about preservation rather than controlling them is the way to build self-confidence and dissolve the fears that will later block spontaneous psychic awareness.

Developing self-acceptance will enable spontaneous thoughts and urges, which you might have otherwise pushed away, to come to the surface. Responding to intuitions requires that you become sensitive to irrational promptings that may come in the form of images and feelings. If you want to express intuition, you need to learn that you can trust the flow of your experiences.

PREPARE A
PLAN OF APPLICATION

What will you do with your psychic ability? If you have no plan for using it, you may feel overwhelmed and afraid. Prepare in advance by thinking how you could use your psychic ability and then get ready to do it.

Trying to develop your ESP out of curiosity alone will not be sufficient. In the long run you bring out your psychic abilities for the simple reason that this is what you have always wanted to do. You will need to create experiments that have a practical application to an area of personal need or motivation.

Get ready to use your psychic ability to overcome obstacles and further develop and express your hidden talents. You might also use this ability to help other people, to bring goodness into the world. God knows we all could use a little goodness in our lives. Develop an agenda based on your needs or on specific purposes for putting your psychic abilities into action. The plan will help you focus your energy as you experiment with the various techniques for developing your psychic abilities within you.

If you get frustrated at work and wish you could get a fresh start in a new career, for example, psychic ability may help you make that move. You may become aware of hidden talents or locate training and employment opportunities more quickly than if you were to read the classifieds in the newspaper. Psychic abilities might give you that added boost you need to go into business for yourself, matching talents with the needs of the marketplace.

Develop some specific goals you wish to work toward and accomplish what you are now prepared to implement. Give your intentions to develop ESP some practical motivation. When you are ready to have the winds blow, raise your sail and get your hand on the rudder. Be prepared!

HOW TO KEEP DEVELOPING

Be sensitive to the energies around you. Pick up more than just an impression of feelings and energies; allow yourself to actually become part of a feeling. See if you can become part of the breeze blowing gently through the trees and allow your energies to flow with that breeze. Let your body soar and feel it fly above the trees. Imagine yourself looking down as you are flying in the clouds. Become a part of your surroundings.

You can become part of anything by being sensitive to its energy. The energy is what makes it what it is.

Index